A PROCESS FOR DEVELOPING A COMMON VOCABULARY IN THE INFORMATION SECURITY AREA

NATO Science for Peace and Security Series

This Series presents the results of scientific meetings supported under the NATO Programme: Science for Peace and Security (SPS).

The NATO SPS Programme supports meetings in the following Key Priority areas: (1) Defence Against Terrorism; (2) Countering other Threats to Security and (3) NATO, Partner and Mediterranean Dialogue Country Priorities. The types of meeting supported are generally "Advanced Study Institutes" and "Advanced Research Workshops". The NATO SPS Series collects together the results of these meetings. The meetings are co-organized by scientists from NATO countries and scientists from NATO's "Partner" or "Mediterranean Dialogue" countries. The observations and recommendations made at the meetings, as well as the contents of the volumes in the Series, reflect those of participants and contributors only; they should not necessarily be regarded as reflecting NATO views or policy.

Advanced Study Institutes (ASI) are high-level tutorial courses to convey the latest developments in a subject to an advanced-level audience.

Advanced Research Workshops (ARW) are expert meetings where an intense but informal exchange of views at the frontiers of a subject aims at identifying directions for future action.

Following a transformation of the programme in 2006 the Series has been re-named and re-organised. Recent volumes on topics not related to security, which result from meetings supported under the programme earlier, may be found in the NATO Science Series.

The Series is published by IOS Press, Amsterdam, and Springer Science and Business Media, Dordrecht, in conjunction with the NATO Public Diplomacy Division.

Sub-Series

A.	Chemistry and Biology	Springer Science and Business Media
B.	Physics and Biophysics	Springer Science and Business Media
C.	Environmental Security	Springer Science and Business Media
D.	Information and Communication Security	IOS Press
E.	Human and Societal Dynamics	IOS Press

http://www.nato.int/science
http://www.springer.com
http://www.iospress.nl

Sub-Series E: Human and Societal Dynamics – Vol. 23   ISSN 1874-6276

A Process for Developing a Common Vocabulary in the Information Security Area

Edited by

Jan von Knop
Heinrich Heine Universität Düsseldorf, Germany

Alexey A. Salnikov
Information Security Institute, Lomonosov University, Moscow, Russia

and

Valeriy V. Yaschenko
Information Security Institute, Lomonosov University, Moscow, Russia

Press

Amsterdam • Berlin • Oxford • Tokyo • Washington, DC

Published in cooperation with NATO Public Diplomacy Division

Proceedings of the NATO Advanced Research Workshop on A Process for Developing
a Common Vocabulary in the Information Security Area
Moscow, Russia
22–23 September 2006

ISBN 978-1-58603-756-7
Library of Congress Control Number: 2007927427

Publisher
IOS Press
Nieuwe Hemweg 6B
1013 BG Amsterdam
Netherlands
fax: +31 20 687 0019
e-mail: order@iospress.nl

Distributor in the UK and Ireland
Gazelle Books Services Ltd.
White Cross Mills
Hightown
Lancaster LA1 4XS
United Kingdom
fax: +44 1524 63232
e-mail: sales@gazellebooks.co.uk

Distributor in the USA and Canada
IOS Press, Inc.
4502 Rachael Manor Drive
Fairfax, VA 22032
USA
fax: +1 703 323 3668
e-mail: iosbooks@iospress.com

LEGAL NOTICE

The publisher is not responsible for the use which might be made of the following information.

PRINTED IN THE NETHERLANDS

A Process for Developing a Common Vocabulary in the Information Security Area
J. von Knop et al. (Eds.)
IOS Press, 2007

Preface

Over the last years there have been tendencies of growing numbers of cyber attacks and a growth of the scale of casualties. Cyber attacks against critically important segments of informational infrastructure, including the systems controlling of transport and hazardous industry are becoming more frequent. Since the attacks are made using the global informational infrastructure they can be organized from any part of the planet. That means that we can only resist them with the help of international cooperation.

Nowadays, the international strategies of counteraction of cyber crime and cyber terrorism are considered at the political level by the leaders of law-enforcement agencies. The scientific part of such strategies must have an adjustable terminology and the conception apparatus. Every scientific investigation, when it involves specialists from different countries, has to start with agreement upon the terminology. There is a need to harmonize different languages in which specialists speak about guaranteeing the information security. These are the languages of the lawyers, insurers, brokers, creators, technicians, law-enforcement structures and standardizations.

There are some dozens of different dictionaries and glossaries in the field of informational security. However even in the use of the basic terms there are disagreements; for example terms like "information security" and "information assurance" are explained in different ways in different countries and no one understands the correlation of the concepts of "cyber terrorism" and "cyber crime". Misunderstanding in explaining the basic concepts influences the second level of the understanding of the terms. Differences in understanding concepts of informational security can exist not only between different countries but between different institutions and organizations in a same country.

List of Participants

Name	Affiliation and Official Address
Vladimir V. BELOKUROV	Lomonosov University, GSP-2 Leninskie Gory, Moscow, 119992, Russia
Jan von KNOP	Heinrich Heine Universität Düsseldorf, Feldstr.14, 40479, Germany
Alexey A. SALNIKOV	Information Security Institute Lomonosov University, 1, Michurinsky Prospect, Moscow, 119192, Russia
Valery V. YASCHENKO	Information Security Institute Lomonosov University, 1, Michurinsky Prospect, Moscow, 119192, Russia
Alexandr GARIN	George C. Marshall European Center for Security Studies, Grainauer Weg 2, Garmisch-Partenkirchen 82467, Germany
Valery A. GOLOVKO	George C. Marshall European Center for Security Studies, Grainauer Weg 2, Garmisch-Partenkirchen 82467, Germany
Tim BREMMERS	Freedom, Security, Justice Independent Consultancy Programme & Project Management Creativity Innovation, Dintel 45, 5032 CN Tilburg, The Netherlands
Paulo Cardoso do AMARAL	School of Economics and Management Catholic University of Portugal, Palma de Cima 1649 023 Lisboa, Portugal
Sanjay GOEL	School of Business Administration 310b University at Albany, State University of New York 1400 Washington Ave. Albany, NY 12222, USA
Brian RANDELL	School of Computing Science University of Newcastle upon Tyne NE1 7RU, UK
Alexandr N. KURBACKIY	Belarusian State University, Prospekt F. Skorini, 4, Minsk, Byelorussia
Vladimir V. SOKOLOV	Information Security Institute Lomonosov University, 1, Michurinsky Prospect, Moscow, 119192, Russia
Dmitriy I. GRIGORIEV	Information Security Institute Lomonosov University, 1, Michurinsky Prospect, Moscow, 119192, Russia
Anatoliy V. LUNIN	INFOTECS Joint Stock Company, 80-5 Leningradsky Prospect, Moscow, 125315, Russia
Yuriy SUHOV	Government Structures' Information Technologies Center, 17 Presnensky Val, Moscow, 123557, Russia
Viktor SOLODOVNIKOV	Russian Federal Cryptography Academy, 30 Yarcevskay street, Moscow, Russia
Anatoliy MALYUK	Information Security School of Moscow Physics and Engineering Institute (State University), 31 Kashirskoe Shosse, Moscow, 115409, Russia
Alexandr V. FEDOROV	The Ministry of Foreign Affairs of Russia, 32/34 Smolenskay-Sennay Ploschad', Moscow, 119200, Russia
Ildus S. NURGALIEV	K.A. Timiryazev Agricultural University – Agricultural Academy, 3 Pryanishnikova street, Moscow, 127550, Russia

Gennadiy V. IVASCHENKO Lomonosov University, GSP-2 Leninskie Gory, Moscow, 119992, Russia

Alexandra V. BELYEVA Citizens Initiative for Internet Policy, 8a Nikitsky Bulvar, Moscow, 121019, Russia

Yuriy V. MALININ Information Systems Academy Stins Coman Group, 126 Pervomaiskay street, Moscow, 105203, Russia

Rinat A. SHARYAPOV Information Security Institute Lomonosov University, 1, Michurinsky Prospect, Moscow, 119192, Russia

Elena V. RYBAKOVA Information Systems Academy Stins Coman Group, 126 Pervomaiskay street, Moscow, 105203, Russia

Victor V. KORNEEV Research Institute "Kvant", 15, 4th Lihachevskij lane, Moscow, 125438, Russia

Georgiy N. BABAKIN Information Security Association, 15, 4th Lihachevskij lane, Moscow, 125438, Russia

Gennadiy V. EMELIYANOV Information Security Association, 15, 4th Lihachevskij lane, Moscow, 125438, Russia

Alexey V. SURIN Public Administration School of Lomonosov University, GSP-2 Leninskie Gory, Moscow, 119992, Russia

Leonid I. LEVKOVICH-MASLUYK "Computerra" Magazine, 8, 2nd Roschinsky Proesd, Moscow, 115419, Russia

Valeriy VASENIN Information Security Institute Lomonosov University, 1, Michurinsky Prospect, Moscow, 119192, Russia

Dmitry V. KONONENKO Federal Security Service of Russian Federation, 1/3 Bolshaya Lubyanka street, Moscow, 101000, Russia

Olga A. ZINOVIEVA Center on Russia and the United States Lomonosov University, GSP-2 Leninskie Gory, Moscow, 119992, Russia

Contents

A Process for Developing a Common Vocabulary in the Information Security Area
J. von Knop et al. (Eds.)
IOS Press, 2007

Opening Speech

Prof. Dr. Vladimir V. BELOKUROV
Vice Rector Lomonosov University, Moscow

This seminar is the first seminar on information security within the cooperation program of the Scientific Committee Russia-NATO.

It is taking place in the Moscow State University because the Interdepartmental Commission on information security of the Security Council of the Russian Federation appointed the MSU as a head organization on humanitarian problems of information security and international cooperation in the field of scientific problems of information security.

Starting from 2001 the Moscow University is actively participating in international conferences, seminars, and different programs on information security. During the past years it became obvious that one of the barriers for further cooperation is a lack of common conceptual framework. Starting form 2004 within the UN such work is being conducted. The development of common conceptual framework is the first issue that needs to be solved within the international cooperation programs in the field of counteraction cyberterrorism. Our seminar is a logical continuation of this activity.

A Process for Developing a Common Vocabulary in the Information Security Area
J. von Knop et al. (Eds.)
IOS Press, 2007

Opening Speech

Prof. Dr. Jan von KNOP
Heinrich Heine Universität Düsseldorf, Germany

Respected Vice Rector Belokurov,
Dear Ladies and Gentlemen,
I would like to thank you very much for the privilege of presenting an opening speech at the NATO-Russia Advanced Research Workshop on "A Process of Developing a Common Vocabulary in the Information Security Area".

It is also an honor for all of us that we can hold this conference at this very prominent place in Moscow at Lomonosov Moscow State University. Please allow me to begin with a few words about the NATO-Russia Advanced Research Workshops. The purpose of these workshops is to contribute to the critical assessment of existing knowledge on important new topics, identify directions for future research and promote close working relationships among scientists from different countries and with different professional experience.

We are very happy that the NATO-Science Committee awarded this topic to Lomonosov Moscow State University due to the outstanding expertise of their scientists in many disciplines of security research.

Dear Ladies and Gentlemen, may I say a few words at the beginning of this workshop about how security research on the internet started and try to locate the position we are in today.

The use of digital information and communication technologies pervades all areas of life in our society and changes the everyday life of each individual. The internet has, with growing speed, become the common property of society and a fundamental work aid for almost all businesses and hundreds of millions of people. However, we have to realize that the network, as well as the computers connected to the network, are still far too vulnerable to attacks, especially since these attacks are becoming more and more complex and numerous. We have also increasingly ascertained that traditional security techniques no longer suffice for being adequately prepared against the potential of attackers.

We all know how important the secure use of modern information technologies is for the future of our countries in a globalize economy. First of all, allow me to present an overview of the history of the emergence of our modern networks.

The current internet developed out of the experimental network ARPANET, which was conceived by a small group of scientists in order to improve the communication possibilities among internationally operating research groups. A further goal was the joint use of large scientific equipment and top class, high capacity computers that were expensive and not available at all locations.

The services and communication protocols that were developed for the ARPANET were primarily oriented around the requirements of scientific communication and the available technical possibilities at that time. Furthermore, the computers had very modest performance capacities from today's standpoint and the telephone lines available for data communication were relatively unreliable.

Descriptions and documentations of the services and networks were scanty because the user group was very homogenous and focused on research. None of the scientists thought about willful disruptions created by users of the net or outsiders. No one ever thought, for example, that there could be hackers. And nobody at all thought that the network could be used for cyber-terrorism, meaning the creation of conditions capable of destabilizing our socio-political or governmental systems or the economy enough to put our national security in question.

Therefore, the security mechanisms in the ARPANET were only directed at dealing with errors of the computers in use, the router, and the software and particularly transmission errors or even a break in the telephone lines.

Nowadays, a communications protocol, somewhat further-developed but with an essentially unchanged philosophy behind it, is being put to use in the completely open internet that is accessible to everyone. The use of the internet has also undergone a fundamental transformation since then. Scientists formerly used the net for the informal exchange of news, for carrying out calculations on super computers, for example. Today we have an immense variety of user categories on the net, citizens, school children, the economy, banks, insurance, administrative offices, governmental institutions, and of course our security and defense services. The types of usage have increased tremendously and extend to commercial, administrative, social and on a large scale also entertainment services.

Of course, it is no surprise that many of these systems connected to the internet today are not well administrated. They are, therefore, vulnerable to attacks from malicious people of various degrees of competence and stubbornness. The motivations of the attackers are also very different.

These groups of people include school children eager to experiment who try to gain control of the computer system either as sport or to prove their abilities, as well as activists with political, economic or even terrorist backgrounds.

The wide range in the intensity and complexity of attacks on the internet as well as the competence of the attackers is one of the greatest challenges facing our society. But on the other hand, our computer systems, networks and organizations provide a very large target due to numerous security gaps. The goal of our efforts must be the creation and implementation of effective defense systems against attackers and the minimization of the vulnerability of our technical and organizational systems.

With the NATO-Russia Advanced Research Workshop "A Process of Developing a Common Vocabulary in the Information Security Area", we want to make an academic contribution to strategic defense against cyber crime and cyber-terrorism in our global information society by dealing with terminology. Every cooperation on an international level that takes place among academics, government officials, diplomats and members of security services and forces requires a consensus about the terminology being used. Harmonizing the terms used in different languages represents an indispensable precondition for the efficient and effective cooperation of specialists at international levels for ensuring information security. Linguistic misunderstandings among politicians, academics, judges or experts – just to mention a few – could have devastating repercussions in the media, the court or defense.

We are very glad that at this NATO-Russia Advanced Research Workshop, academic contributions will be heard from top class, internationally active experts on the topic of terminology in the area of information security. I wish the conference "A Process of Developing a Common Vocabulary in the Information Security Area" a successful progression.

A Process for Developing a Common Vocabulary in the Information Security Area
J. von Knop et al. (Eds.)
IOS Press, 2007

Legal Groundwork for Information Security and Conceptual Framework

Prof. Dr. Anatoliy A. STRELTSOV
Head of Department, Security Consul of Russian Federation

An important component of providing national security in the context of information society development is legal regulation of public relations related to countering threats of information security. Legal regulation is a basis for legal groundwork of information security. Legal groundwork acts as legal mechanisms of impact on public relations in order to counteract security threats and is being developed in an interacting process between law, as a tool for regulating public relations, and state, as main subject for counteracting its security threats.

Threats of information security represent a complex of conditions and factors that have a negative effect on, in the first place, safety of national interests objects in the field of information and, in particular, on key objects of society's information infrastructure.

Important features of considerable part of information security threats are:

- Cross border character of their exposure related to interconnectivity of national information infrastructures within global information infrastructure;
- Complexity and lack of transparency of algorithms in functioning of information and communication systems, which create conditions for intensive development of means of destructive information impact on public information infrastructure objects called "information weapon".

Taking into account that no state alone can successfully counteract the given threats, the development of effective mechanisms for international cooperation, which are based on international agreements between engaged states and their entities and lie at the essence of international information security, plays crucial role.

The collection of these documents shall create a basis for forming legal groundwork for international information security and, in parallel, for development of system of international agreements that already operate in the field of information security and form dogmatic of international humanitarian law and international security law.

The first step in solving this issue can be a development of multilingual conceptual framework that will allow both politicians and specialists, working in the field of legislation, law enforcement, and prosecution, to have a common approach to legal regulation that represents a complex of public relations which need to be influenced by law for ensuring national and international information security.

The creation of such conceptual framework will contribute to forming necessary conditions both for harmonizing national legislations and for developing international agreements aimed to regulate relations in the field of providing information security of a single state and international community as a whole.

At bottom of multilingual conceptual framework it would be reasonable to put legal regulation in the area of expertise structure. In this case the conceptual framework structure will include four main concept sections describing:

- Information public relations;
- Objects of national interests in the fields of information security;
- Threats to security objects of national interests;
- Counteraction against these threats.

Thereafter

1. While developing conceptual framework section related to "information relations" it will be reasonable to proceed assuming that information relations involve legally regulated public relations that emerge in process of interaction between subjects to fulfill subjects' interests.

Five main groups of information relations can be distinguished:

- Commodity-money relations in which information in form of a message acts as a product, service or an object of intellectual property law;
- Spiritual relations where information in form of data acts as tool for impact on psychological state of a subject;
- Relations in the field of social and state control in which information in form of data and messages acts as a tool for subjects identification, for regulating subjects activity;
- Relations in the field of technical and technological systems control in which information in form of messages acts as a tool for providing coordinated functioning of separate systems components;
- Relations related to everyday communication between individuals where information in form of data acts as a tool for subjects' self-improvement, for their informational "enrichment".

The analysis of the given relations groups shows that they are produced by following subjects interests implemented in information sphere:

- Free possession of information;
- Sharing a part of information with some subjects;
- Maintain information in abeyance for other subjects.

Thus, taking into consideration role and place of information in human life, we can presume that his interests related to information are determined by a necessity to adapt to living conditions in natural and social environment and consist of obtaining the needed information, information exchange with other humans and keeping part of information in obscurity from other individuals. The last case provides a certain degree of independence of individual from other people and increases conform of his existence.

Society interests related to information are determined by a need to support social stability, provide better living conditions for society members (citizens) and to secure social development. The interests are determined by possession of institutional social formations of the needed information, information exchange between members of social formations, keeping part of information that members of this social formation obscure for others. This increases stability of the given social formation functioning in context of common conflict of its interests with interests of other social formations.

Related to information state interests are determined by a need effectively to fulfill the function of society control, providing its security and development. Its interests lie in state bodies' possession of certain information, information transmission to citizens, social formations and keeping information, which release may damage state performance, obscure to unauthorized people.

Thereby actions to obtain messages are accomplished through their search, obtaining, and storage. Actions to obtain data are accomplished through message use to obtain data (for reading). Actions to transmit data are realized through data transformation into message (message production), message transmission and dissemination. Actions to keep information obscure to other subjects are accomplished through taking special measures to prevent unauthorized inspection of subject's messages and through subject's constraint to form such messages.

In order to implement its interests subject is forced to cooperate with other subjects, giving these relations a certain form, i.e. adhere to certain rules of relation implementation. These rules depend on level of information infrastructure development and on means that the information infrastructure may provide to subject to accomplish its interests.

In civil relations this cooperation acquires a shape of a deal with service as its objects. In public relations it acquires a shape of a demand or request.

Thus, in civil relations cooperation for the purpose of information search may be practiced as a deal. The deal's content includes rendering an intermediary service for search of messages that possess certain features (message saving mode, spheres of material or spiritual life of the society described in the message, level of theoretic generalization of data, language of data encryption, etc.), enabling of independent search in message complex that is owned by the subject. A social result of such cooperation can be a determination message storage place that meets search requirements, determination of subject, which owns this message, obtaining an authorization for message access or subject's rejection in providing such an access or failure to determine a storage place for desired messages.

The cooperation for the purpose of message receiving can be practiced as a deal, its, but cooperation for the purpose to store messages is practices as a service for providing safety to stored messages. The social result of given cooperation will be receiving of needed messages, saving physical features of tangible medium on which message is saved and, therefore, a possibility content includes rendering an intermediary service for search of messages to study message content.

The cooperation for purpose of message use for obtaining data can be conducted as a deal. The deal's content includes providing a possibility to study messages in which subject is interested in. The social result of given cooperation involves message transformation into data that is reflected in "informational model" of the subject.

Cooperation for purpose of data transmission (circulation) can be practiced as a deal that includes providing service for securing message that contains transmitted data on tangible medium, for transmission (dissemination) of the message to certain subjects or to indefinitely large number of subjects through different means (mail delivery, agitation and propaganda, advertisement of billboards, message dissemination through radio, television, other mass media, on Internet web-sites, etc.). Social result of such interaction involves message delivery to addressees or addressees' introduction with message content that presumes changes in their behavior under certain circumstances.

In public relations cooperation is conducted for the purpose of meeting individual's and society's interests related to information that state posses and state interests related to information that is possessed by individual, organization, and local authorities that lie at the basis of civil society.

Individual's and society's interests related to information possessed by state are directed/aimed to obtaining information needed for conducting control over the state's activity, forming the right behavior, evaluating the situation formed in the most important fields of social life and for passing/delegating to the state and its institutions the information needed for performing by the state the functions assigned/placed on it.

The interaction between an individual or an organization with the state institutions with the goal of obtaining or passing the necessary information can be realized in the form of addresses. The interaction between the state institutions with an individual and an organization with the goal of obtaining the information possessed by them can be realized in the form of a demand/requirement/requisition in cases when providing information is ordered by legal regulations or in the form of a notification, in cases when publishing of the information by state institutions is ordered/prescribed by legal regulations. This interaction may be realized in the form of a refusal to provide information in cases mentioned by the law. The condition for the realization of interests of the subjects of social relations, whose object is information, is stable and safe functioning of the informational infrastructure in the society. The composition/contents of this infrastructure and the essence of the social relations, occurring in connection with it's functioning/use, are determined/defined/shaped by the level of the society development, its economic potential, the ability to implement the results of scientific and technological progress (R&D?). One can single out the following components in modern informational infrastructure: organizational/managing, technological and informational. Organizational/managing component includes: bodies and service that provide stable functioning of the technological and informational components of the infrastructure, mass-media, and organizations that provide informational services. For its part, the technological component includes: nets and objects of communication; telecommunications; means of automation of social and technological processes management, automation of data processing; computer nets and systems. And informational component consists of informational systems, including library, archive and museum funds.

Subject's interests connected with the use of informational infrastructure, are realized through establishing interaction with other subjects with the goal of receiving communication services, gaining an opportunity to use messages, stored in information systems, as well as using means of automation of management and data processing and computer systems for processing information. The social result of these interactions is the increase of main information activity realization quality.

The second characteristic of social relations, that are the subject of legal regulation/component of information security, is there connection with the objects of national interests in the information field.

2. While creating/compiling the conceptual framework related to **the objects of national interests,** it is expedient to proceed on/with an assumption/fact that national interests are a balanced entity of individual's social interests, interests of the society and state, the realization of which serves as a guarantee of existence, security and stable development of the nation in concrete historical conditions. This entity has to be recognized by the state and provided by legal regulation base. The content of national interests in the information sphere are fixed in some form in the legal acts or in the political documents, passed in the authorized state bodies or officials.

Analysis of the content of the national interests in the information sphere shows that their main objects is information in the form of facts/data and messages, informational infrastructure and the legal status in the information field of an individual and subjects representing society and state.

Information in the form of facts/data is an object of individual's social interests and in a certain degree an object of society and state interests, because it predetermines the individual's behavior in the society, his observing certain established code/rules of interaction with other people, his attitude to the society as a social "milieu".

The social interests of an individual lie, on the one hand, in a free accumulation and use of the data/facts, needed for individual and social adaptation, which allows him to preserve the necessary amount/degree of independence on other persons in solving personal problems and therefore building their private and partially social life. On the other hand, these social interests lie in the freedom to preserve/keep certain part of possessed data secret/unknown for other people, organizations and social institutions. Taking into consideration that data are the result of psychic activity of the person's brain and are part of the inner world of an individual, they are realized in his social interests, in the interests of the society and the state, and consequently in the national interests in the form (which takes the form) of freedom of individual's psychic activity and in the form of cultural invariants supported by the individual. Only on condition of freedom of psychic activity an individual can perform volitional actions and take responsibility for them.

Among the abundance of data, that constitute the object of society's interests, a special place is occupied by cultural invariants. They are the spiritual basis for the existence of a nation as a social entity. Data about the objects and ideas that form these cultural invariants are known to every member of the society, but their subjective value might vary. As an integral entity the society is interested in the high significance of cultural values that unify the members of the society. Here (at that point) the interest of the society and the individual, who considers himself/herself to be a part of the given society, coincides. Otherwise the society may simply cease to exist, as it happened with the Soviet Union.

National cultural values in the modern society in many aspects are the manifestation of common to all humans/manhood ethical values in certain/particular historical and social conditions. Among such ethical values there are good and evil, justice, duty, conscience, happiness, meaning of life, moral ideal. Transforming into national cultural values they become the essence of principles and conduct/behavioral norms, other cultural universalities of the nation. They appeal to individual's free choice and are substantiated by the inner (within the personality) more profound (deeper) control forms (conscience, guilt, repentance/remorse etc.)

National cultural values occupy a significant part of public consciousness, which is an entity of socially meaningful ideals, ideas, points of view, studies and theories, wishes, habits and traditions, perceived by individuals and corresponding to objective demands of the society. Within the structure of the social consciousness one can distinguish individual social consciousness, which is formed by the data needed for individual's adaptation to the changes in social reality through participation in the activities of different social communities. It reflects social life/existence through the prism of individual's interests and feelings/emotions One can also distinguish mass social consciousness, which is formed by the total block of data, possessed by members of the society and reflecting typical for the time frames of mind and expectations of the people of different classes and social groups, which manifest itself in public opinion. Depending on the sphere of social life, reflected in the social consciousness one can distinguish its different forms: political, legal, religious, and esthetic social consciousness, and science. Each of these forms of social consciousness pertain their own national cultural values, the preservation of which serve the unification of the nation.

The data can represent an object of the state's interests in case they determine the performance of its functions. Among these data are the ones that can damage state interests. The government is keen on keeping these data unknown to those whom it does not concern.

Information in the form of data becomes an object of national interests due to the fact that it contains in the encoded way the data on/about cultural values, allows to save and accumulate them, and enables/gives an opportunity to interested subjects to acknowledge them (to get acquainted with them). In reference books the notion "to save" is defined as "to keep, to retain, to maintain, to preserve, to protect from damage, violation, change". And the notion "to accumulate" is defined as "to gather in certain quantity permanently increasing or adding, to take, to purchase something". Proceeding on this/therefore the content of the social function of preserving information in the form of data related to cultural values is in protecting the above mentioned data from damage, destruction and also from alternation/change, and the functions of saving is in increasing their quantity.

Informational infrastructure becomes an object of national interests in connection with fact that it is a means of increasing the efficiency of realization of individual's social interests, interests of the society and the state. In reference books the notion "infrastructure" is defined as "economic complex, that is providing services to industry and is providing the functioning of the society" Thus informational infrastructure as an integral part of the infrastructure of the society is/represents a complex of economic branches, which provide services to information activity, that is the activity, aimed/directed to the realization of the interests of subjects (individual, society and state) in the informational field, connected with the possession of necessary information, with passing/sharing this information with other subjects, as well as with keeping the remaining part of this information unknown to these subjects.

The information activity consists of search, receiving, keeping/preservation, transfer/sharing, production, use/application and spreading the information in the form of data. For the purpose of efficiency increase of informational activity the subjects can use informational infrastructure of the society. While transferring and receiving information they use means of communication; for storage, production and use of information – means of information, and for its mass/wide spreading – mass media, including book publishing and global info-telecommunication systems. Taking all this into consideration the informational infrastructure of the society forms an entity of three parts – infrastructures of communication, information and mass information.

A Process for Developing a Common Vocabulary in the Information Security Area
J. von Knop et al. (Eds.)
IOS Press, 2007

Basic Concepts and Taxonomy of Dependable and Secure Computing[1]

Algirdas AVIZIENIS, *Fellow, IEEE,* Jean-Claude LAPRIE, Brian RANDELL,
and Carl LANDWEHR, *Senior Member, IEEE*

Abstract. This paper gives the main definitions relating to dependability, a generic concept including as special case such attributes as reliability, availability, safety, integrity, maintainability, etc. Security brings in concerns for confidentiality, in addition to availability and integrity. Basic definitions are given first. They are then commented upon, and supplemented by additional definitions, which address the threats to dependability and security (faults, errors, failures), their attributes, and the means for their achievement (fault prevention, fault tolerance, fault removal, fault forecasting). The aim is to explicate a set of general concepts, of relevance across a wide range of situations and, therefore, helping communication and cooperation among a number of scientific and technical communities, including ones that are concentrating on particular types of system, of system failures, or of causes of system failures.

Keywords. Dependability, security, trust, faults, errors, failures, vulnerabilities, attacks, fault tolerance, fault removal, fault forecasting.

1. Introduction

This paper aims to give precise definitions characterizing the various concepts that come into play when addressing the dependability and security of computing and communication systems. Clarifying these concepts is surprisingly difficult when we discuss systems in which there are uncertainties about system boundaries. Furthermore, the very complexity of systems (and their specification) is often a major problem, the determination of possible causes or consequences of failure can be a very subtle process, and there are (fallible) provisions for preventing faults from causing failures.

Dependability is first introduced as a global concept that subsumes the usual attributes of reliability, availability, safety, integrity, maintainability, etc. The consideration of security brings in concerns for confidentiality, in addition to availability and integrity. The basic definitions are then commented upon and supplemented by additional definitions. **Boldface** characters are used when a term is defined, while *italic* characters are an invitation to focus the reader's attention.

This paper can be seen as an attempt to document a minimum consensus on concepts within various specialties in order to facilitate fruitful technical interactions; in addition, we hope that it will be suitable 1) for use by other bodies (including standardization organizations) and 2) for educational purposes. Our concern is with the concepts: words are only of interest because they unequivocally label concepts and enable ideas and viewpoints to be shared. An important issue, for which we believe a

---

[1] Originally published in *IEEE Transactions on Dependable and Secure Computing*, **vol. 1**, No. 1, January-March 2004, 11–33.

consensus has not yet emerged, concerns the measures of dependability and security; this issue will necessitate further elaboration before being documented consistently with the other aspects of the taxonomy that is presented here.

The paper has no pretension of documenting the state-of-the-art. Thus, together with the focus on concepts, we do not address implementation issues such as can be found in standards, for example, in [30] for safety or [32] for security.

The dependability and security communities have followed distinct, but convergent paths: 1) dependability has realized that restriction to nonmalicious faults was addressing only a part of the problem, 2) security has realized that the main focus that was put in the past on confidentiality needed to be augmented with concerns for integrity and for availability (they have been always present in the definitions, but did not receive as much attention as confidentiality). The paper aims to bring together the common strands of dependability and security although, for reasons of space limitation, confidentiality is not given the attention it deserves.

Preceding Work and Goals for the Future. The origin of this effort dates back to 1980, when a joint committee on "Fundamental Concepts and Terminology" was formed by the TC on Fault-Tolerant Computing of the IEEE CS and the IFIP WG 10.4 "Dependable Computing and Fault Tolerance." Seven position papers were presented in 1982 at a special session of FTCS-12 [21], and a synthesis was presented at FTCS-15 in 1985 [40] which is a direct predecessor of this paper, but provides a much less detailed classification, in particular of dependability threats and attributes.

Continued intensive discussions led to the 1992 book *Dependability: Basic Concepts and Terminology* [41], which contained a 34-page English text with an eight-page glossary and its translations into French, German, Italian, and Japanese. The principal innovations were the addition of *security* as an attribute and of the class of intentional *malicious faults* in the taxonomy of faults. Many concepts were refined and elaborated.

The next major step was the recognition of security as a composite of the attributes of *confidentiality*, *integrity*, and *availability* and the addition of the class of *intentional nonmalicious faults, together with an analysis of the problems of inadequate system specifications* [42], though this account provided only a summary classification of dependability threats.

The present paper represents the results of a continuous effort since 1995 to expand, refine, and simplify the taxonomy of dependable and secure computing. It is also our goal to make the taxonomy readily available to practitioners and students of the field; therefore, this paper is self-contained and does not require reading of the above mentioned publications. The major new contributions are:

1. *The relationship between dependability and security* is clarified (Section 2.3).
2. *A quantitative definition of dependability* is introduced (Section 2.3).
3. *The criterion of capability* is introduced in the classification of human-made nonmalicious faults (Sections 3.2.1 and 3.2.3), enabling the consideration of *competence*.
4. *The discussion of malicious faults* is extensively updated (Section 3.2.4).
5. *Service failures* (Section 3.3.1) are distinguished from dependability failures (Section 3.3.3): The latter are recognized when service failures over a period of time are too frequent or too severe.
6. *Dependability issues of the development process* are explicitly incorporated into the taxonomy, including partial and complete *development failures* (Section 3.3.2).

7.   The concept of *dependability is related to dependence and trust* (Section 4.2), and compared with three recently introduced similar concepts, including survivability, trustworthiness, high-confidence systems (Section 4.4).

After the present extensive iteration, what future opportunities and challenges can we foresee that will prompt the evolution of the taxonomy? Certainly, we recognize the desirability of further:

- expanding the discussion of security, for example to cover techniques for protecting confidentiality, establishing authenticity, etc.,
- analyzing issues of trust and the allied topic of risk management, and
- searching for unified measures of dependability and security.

We expect that some challenges will come unexpectedly (perhaps as so-called "emergent properties," such as those of the HAL computer in Arthur C. Clarke's "2001: A Space Odyssey") as the complexity of man-machine systems that we can build exceeds our ability to comprehend them. Other challenges are easier to predict:

1.   New technologies (nanosystems, biochips, chemical and quantum computing, etc.) and new concepts of man-machine systems (ambient computing, nomadic computing, grid computing, etc.) will require continued attention to their specific dependability issues.
2.   The problems of complex human-machine interactions (including user interfaces) remain a challenge that is becoming very critical – the means to improve their dependability and security need to be identified and incorporated.
3.   The dark side of human nature causes us to anticipate new forms of maliciousness that will lead to more forms of malicious faults and, hence, requirements for new defenses as well.

In view of the above challenges and because of the continuing and unnecessarily confusing introduction of purportedly "new" concepts to describe the same means, attributes, and threats, the most urgent goal for the future is to keep the taxonomy complete to the extent that this is possible, but at the same time as simple and well-structured as our abilities allow.

2. The Basic Concepts

In this section, we present a basic set of definitions that will be used throughout the entire discussion of the taxonomy of dependable and secure computing. The definitions are general enough to cover the entire range of computing and communication systems, from individual logic gates to networks of computers with human operators and users. In what follows, we focus mainly on computing and communications systems, but our definitions are also intended in large part to be of relevance to **computer-based systems**, i.e., systems which also encompass the humans and organizations that provide the immediate environment of the computing and communication systems of interest.

2.1 System Function, Behavior, Structure, and Service

A **system** in our taxonomy is an entity that interacts with other entities, i.e., other systems, including hardware, software, humans, and the physical world with its natural phenomena. These other systems are the **environment** of the given system. The **system boundary** is the common frontier between the system and its environment.

Computing and communication systems are characterized by fundamental properties: *functionality, performance, dependability and security*, and *cost*. Other important system properties that affect dependability and security include usability, manageability, and adaptability – detailed consideration of these issues is beyond the scope of this paper. The **function** of such a system is what the system is intended to do and is described by the **functional specification** in terms of functionality and performance. The **behavior** of a system is what the system does to implement its function and is described by a sequence of states. The **total state** of a given system is the set of the following states: computation, communication, stored information, interconnection, and physical condition.

The **structure** of a system is what enables it to generate the behavior. From a structural viewpoint, a system is composed of a set of **components** bound together in order to interact, where each component is another system, etc. The recursion stops when a component is considered to be **atomic:** Any further internal structure cannot be discerned, or is not of interest and can be ignored. Consequently, the total state of a system is the set of the (external) states of its atomic components.

The **service** delivered by a system (in its role as a **provider**) is its behavior as it is perceived by its user(s); a **user** is another system that receives service from the provider. The part of the provider's system boundary where service delivery takes place is the provider's **service interface**. The part of the provider's total state that is perceivable at the service interface is its **external state**; the remaining part is its **internal state**. The delivered service is a sequence of the provider's external states. We note that a system may sequentially or simultaneously be a provider and a user with respect to another system, i.e., deliver service to and receive service from that other system. The interface of the user at which the user receives service is the **use interface**.

We have up to now used the singular for function and service. A system generally implements more than one function, and delivers more than one service. Function and service can be thus seen as composed of function items and of service items. For the sake of simplicity, we shall simply use the plural – functions, services – when it is necessary to distinguish several function or service items.

2.2 The Threats to Dependability and Security: Failures, Errors, Faults

Correct service is delivered when the service implements the system function. A **service failure**, often abbreviated here to **failure**, is an event that occurs when the delivered service deviates from correct service. A service fails either because it does not comply with the functional specification, or because this specification did not adequately describe the system function. A service failure is a **transition** from correct service to incorrect service, i.e., to not implementing the system function. The period of delivery of incorrect service is a **service outage**. The transition from incorrect service to correct service is a **service restoration**. The deviation from correct service may assume different forms that are called **service failure modes** and are ranked according to failure severities. A detailed taxonomy of failure modes is presented in Section 3.

Since a service is a sequence of the system's external states, a service failure means that at least one (or more) external state of the system deviates from the correct service state. The deviation is called an *error*. The adjudged or hypothesized cause of an error is called a **fault**. Faults can be internal or external of a system. The prior presence of a **vulnerability**, i.e., an internal fault that enables an external fault to harm the system, is necessary for an external fault to cause an error and possibly subsequent failure(s). In most cases, a fault first causes an error in the service state of a component that is a part of the internal state of the system and the external state is not immediately affected.

For this reason, the definition of an **error** is the part of the total state of the system that may lead to its subsequent service failure. It is important to note that many errors do not reach the system's external state and cause a failure. A fault is **active** when it causes an error, otherwise it is **dormant**.

When the functional specification of a system includes a set of several functions, the failure of one or more of the services implementing the functions may leave the system in a **degraded mode** that still offers a subset of needed services to the user. The specification may identify several such modes, e.g., slow service, limited service, emergency service, etc. Here, we say that the system has suffered a **partial failure** of its functionality or performance. Development failures and dependability failures that are discussed in Section 3.3 also can be partial failures.

2.3 Dependability, Security, and Their Attributes

The original definition of **dependability** is the ability to deliver service that can justifiably be trusted. This definition stresses the need for justification of trust. The alternate definition that provides the criterion for deciding if the service is dependable is the **dependability** of a system is the ability to avoid service failures that are more frequent and more severe than is acceptable.

It is usual to say that the dependability of a system should suffice for the dependence being placed on that system. The **dependence** of system A on system B, thus, represents the extent to which system A's dependability is (or would be) affected by that of System B. The concept of dependence leads to that of **trust**, which can very conveniently be defined as *accepted dependence*.

As developed over the past three decades, dependability is an integrating concept that encompasses the following attributes:

- **availability:** readiness for correct service.
- **reliability:** continuity of correct service.
- **safety:** absence of catastrophic consequences on the user(s) and the environment.
- **integrity:** absence of improper system alterations.
- **maintainability:** ability to undergo modifications and repairs.

When addressing security, an additional attribute has great prominence, **confidentiality**, i.e., the absence of unauthorized disclosure of information. **Security** is a composite of the attributes of confidentiality, integrity, and availability, requiring the concurrent existence of 1) availability for authorized actions only, 2) confidentiality, and 3) integrity with "improper" meaning "unauthorized."

Fig. 1 summarizes the relationship between dependability and security in terms of their principal attributes. The picture should *not* be interpreted as indicating that, for example, security developers have no interest in maintainability, or that there has been no research at all in the dependability field related to confidentiality – rather it indicates where the main balance of interest and activity lies in each case.

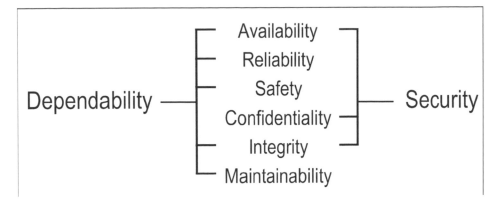

Fig. 1. Dependability and security attributes.

The **dependability and security specification** of a system must include the requirements for the attributes in terms of the acceptable frequency and severity of service failures for specified classes of faults and a given use environment. One or more attributes may not be required at all for a given system.

2.4 The Means to Attain Dependability and Security

Over the course of the past 50 years many means have been developed to attain the various attributes of dependability and security. Those means can be grouped into four major categories:

- **Fault prevention** means to prevent the occurrence or introduction of faults.
- **Fault tolerance** means to avoid service failures in the presence of faults.
- **Fault removal** means to reduce the number and severity of faults.
- **Fault forecasting** means to estimate the present number, the future incidence, and the likely consequences of faults.

Fault prevention and fault tolerance aim to provide the ability to deliver a service that can be trusted, while fault removal and fault forecasting aim to reach confidence in that ability by justifying that the functional and the dependability and security specifications are adequate and that the system is likely to meet them.

2.5 Summary: The Dependability and Security Tree

The schema of the complete taxonomy of dependable and secure computing as outlined in this section is shown in Fig. 2.

3. The Threats to Dependability and Security

3.1 System Life Cycle: Phases and Environments

In this section, we present the taxonomy of threats that may affect a system during its entire life. The **life cycle** of a system consists of two phases: *development* and *use*.

The development phase includes all activities from presentation of the user's initial concept to the decision that the system has passed all acceptance tests and is ready to deliver service in its user's environment. During the development phase, the

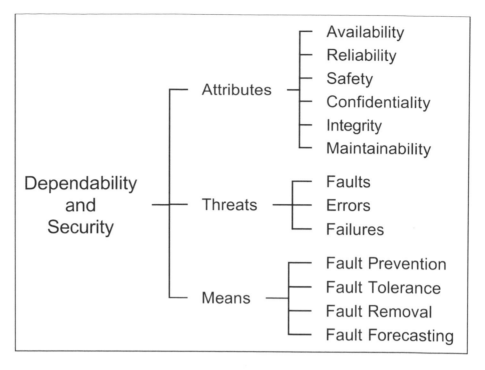

Fig. 2. Dependability and security tree.

system interacts with the development environment and *development faults* may be introduced into the system by the environment. The **development environment** of a system consists of the following elements:

1. the *physical world* with its natural phenomena,
2. *human developers*, some possibly lacking competence or having malicious objectives,
3. *development tools*: software and hardware used by the developers to assist them in the development process,
4. *production and test facilities*.

The use phase of a system's life begins when the system is accepted for use and starts the delivery of its services to the users. Use consists of alternating periods of correct service delivery (to be called **service delivery**), service outage, and service shutdown. A *service outage* is caused by a service failure. It is the period when incorrect service (including no service at all) is delivered at the service interface. A **service shutdown** is an intentional halt of service by an authorized entity. **Maintenance** actions may take place during all three periods of the use phase.

During the use phase, the system interacts with its *use environment* and may be adversely affected by faults originating in it. The **use environment** consists of the following elements:

1. *the physical world* with its natural phenomena;
2. *administrators* (including maintainers): entities (humans or other systems) that have the authority to manage, modify, repair and use the system; some authorized humans may lack competence or have malicious objectives;

3. *users*: entities (humans or other systems) that receive service from the system at their use interfaces;
4. *providers*: entities (humans or other systems) that deliver services to the system at its use interfaces;
5. *the infrastructure*: entities that provide specialized services to the system, such as information sources (e.g., time, GPS, etc.), communication links, power sources, cooling airflow, etc.
6. *intruders*: malicious entities (humans and other systems) that attempt to exceed any authority they might have and alter service or halt it, alter the system's functionality or performance, or to access confidential information. Examples include hackers, vandals, corrupt insiders, agents of hostile governments or organizations, and malicious software.

As used here, the term **maintenance**, following common usage, includes not only repairs, but also all modifications of the system that take place during the use phase of system life. Therefore, maintenance is a development process, and the preceding discussion of development applies to maintenance as well. The various forms of maintenance are summarized in Fig. 3.

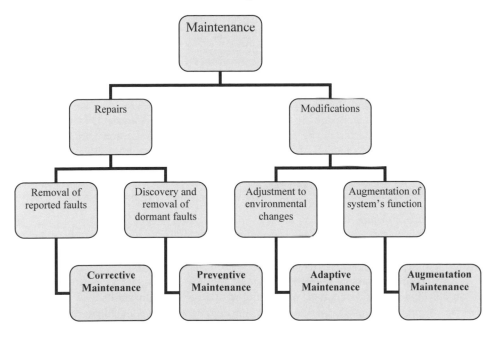

Fig. 3. The various forms of maintenance.

It is noteworthy that repair and fault tolerance are related concepts; the distinction between fault tolerance and maintenance in this paper is that maintenance involves the participation of an external agent, e.g., a repairman, test equipment, remote reloading of software. Furthermore, repair is part of fault removal (during the use phase), and fault forecasting usually considers repair situations. In fact, repair can be seen as a fault tolerance activity within a larger system that includes the system being repaired and the people and other systems that perform such repairs.

3.2 Faults

3.2.1 A Taxonomy of Faults

All faults that may affect a system during its life are classified according to eight basic viewpoints, leading to the *elementary fault classes*, as shown in Fig. 4.

If all combinations of the eight elementary fault classes were possible, there would be 256 different *combined fault classes*. However, not all criteria are applicable to all fault classes; for example, natural faults cannot be classified by objective, intent, and capability. *We have identified 31 likely combinations*; they are shown in Fig. 5.

More combinations may be identified in the future. The combined fault classes of Fig. 5 are shown to belong to three major partially overlapping groupings:

- **development faults** that include all fault classes occurring during development,
- **physical faults** that include all fault classes that affect hardware,
- **interaction faults** that include all external faults.

The boxes at the bottom of Fig. 5a identify the names of some illustrative fault classes.

Knowledge of all possible fault classes allows the user to decide which classes should be included in a dependability and security specification. Next, we comment on the fault classes that are shown in Fig. 5. Fault numbers (1 to 31) will be used to relate the discussion to Fig. 5.

3.2.2 On Natural Faults

Natural faults (11-15) are physical (hardware) faults that are caused by natural phenomena without human participation. We note that humans also can cause physical faults (6-10, 16-23); these are discussed below. *Production defects* (11) are natural faults that originate during development. During operation the natural faults are either *internal* (12-13), due to natural processes that cause physical deterioration, or *external* (14-15), due to natural processes that originate outside the system boundaries and cause physical interference by penetrating the hardware boundary of the system (radiation, etc.) or by entering via use interfaces (power transients, noisy input lines, etc.).

3.2.3 On Human-Made Faults

The definition of human-made faults (that result from human actions) includes absence of actions when actions should be performed, i.e., **omission faults**, or simply **omissions**. Performing wrong actions leads to **commission faults**.

The two basic classes of human-made faults are distinguished by the *objective* of the developer or of the humans interacting with the system during its use:

- *Malicious faults*, introduced during either system development with the objective to cause harm to the system during its use (5-6), or directly during use (22-25).
- *Nonmalicious faults* (1-4, 7-21, 26-31), introduced without malicious objectives.

We consider nonmalicious faults first. They can be partitioned according to the developer's intent:

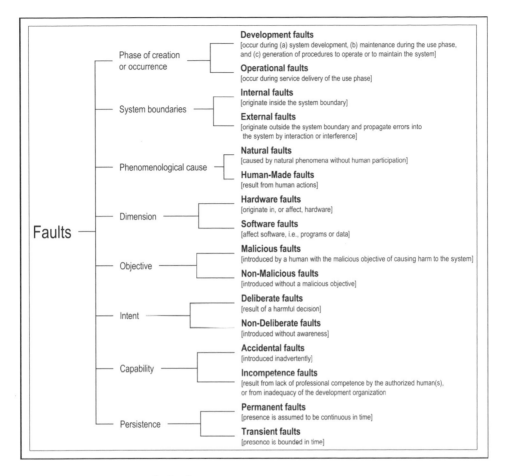

Fig. 4. The elementary fault classes.

- *nondeliberate* faults that are due to *mistakes*, that is, *unintended actions* of which the developer, operator, maintainer, etc. is not aware (1, 2, 7, 8, 16-18, 26-28);
- *deliberate* faults that are due to *bad decisions*, that is, *intended actions* that are wrong and cause faults (3, 4, 9, 10, 19-21, 29-31).

Deliberate, nonmalicious, development faults (3, 4, 9, 10) result generally from trade offs, either 1) aimed at preserving acceptable performance, at facilitating system utilization, or 2) induced by economic considerations. Deliberate, nonmalicious interaction faults (19-21, 29-31) may result from the action of an operator either aimed at overcoming an unforeseen situation, or deliberately violating an operating procedure without having realized the possibly damaging consequences of this action. Deliberate, nonmalicious faults are often recognized as faults only *after* an unacceptable system behavior; thus, a failure has ensued. The developer(s) or operator(s) did not realize at the time that the consequence of their decision was a fault.

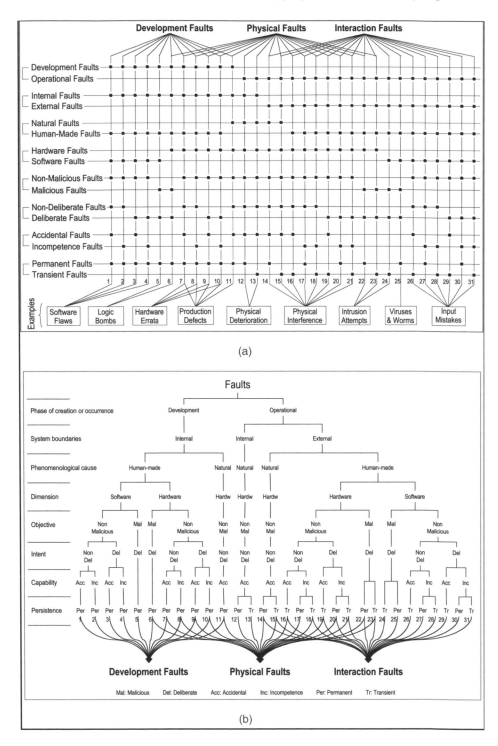

Fig. 5. The classes of combined faults (a) Matrix representation. (b) Tree representation.

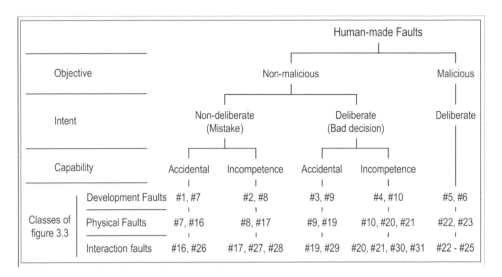

Fig. 6. Classification of human-made faults.

It is usually considered that both mistakes and bad decisions are *accidental*, as long as they are not made with malicious objectives. However, *not all* mistakes and bad decisions by nonmalicious persons are accidents. Some very harmful mistakes and very bad decisions are made by persons who lack professional competence to do the job they have undertaken. A complete fault taxonomy should not conceal this cause of faults; therefore, we introduce a further partitioning of nonmalicious human-made faults into 1) *accidental faults*, and 2) *incompetence faults*. The structure of this taxonomy of human-made faults is shown in Fig. 6.

The question of how to recognize incompetence faults becomes important when a mistake or a bad decision has consequences that lead to economic losses, injuries, or loss of human lives. In such cases, independent professional judgment by a board of inquiry or legal proceedings in a court of law are likely to be needed to decide if professional malpractice was involved.

Thus far, the discussion of incompetence faults has dealt with individuals. However, human-made efforts have failed because a team or an entire organization did not have the organizational competence to do the job. A good example of organizational incompetence is the development failure of the AAS system, that was intended to replace the aging air traffic control systems in the USA [67].

Nonmalicious development faults can exist in hardware and in software. In hardware, especially in microprocessors, some development faults are discovered after production has started [5]. Such faults are called "errata" and are listed in specification updates. The finding of errata typically continues throughout the life of the processors; therefore, new specification updates are issued periodically. Some development faults are introduced because human-made tools are faulty.

Off-the-shelf (OTS) components are inevitably used in system design. The use of OTS components introduces additional problems. They may come with known development faults and may contain unknown faults as well (bugs, vulnerabilities, undiscovered errata, etc.). Their specifications may be incomplete or even incorrect. This problem is especially serious when *legacy* OTS components are used that come from previously designed and used systems, and must be retained in the new system because of the user's needs.

Some development faults affecting software can cause **software aging** [27], i.e., progressively accrued error conditions resulting in performance degradation or complete failure. Examples are memory bloating and leaking, unterminated threads, unreleased file-locks, data corruption, storage space fragmentation, and accumulation of round-off errors [10].

3.2.4 On Malicious Faults

Malicious human-made faults are introduced with the malicious objective to alter the functioning of the system during use. Because of the objective, classification according to intent and capability is not applicable. The goals of such faults are: 1) to disrupt or halt service, causing denials of service; 2) to access confidential information; or 3) to improperly modify the system. They are grouped into two classes:

1. **Malicious logic faults** that encompass development faults (5,6) such as *Trojan horses*, logic or timing *bombs*, and *trapdoors*, as well as operational faults (25) such as *viruses*, *worms*, or *zombies*. Definitions for these faults [39], [55] are given in Fig. 7.

2. **Intrusion attempts** that are operational external faults (22-24). The external character of intrusion attempts does not exclude the possibility that they may be performed by system operators or administrators who are exceeding their rights, and intrusion attempts may use physical means to cause faults: power fluctuation, radiation, wire-tapping, heating/cooling, etc.

What is colloquially known as an "exploit" is in essence a software script that will exercise a system vulnerability and allow an intruder to gain access to, and sometimes control of, a system. In the terms defined here, invoking the exploit is an operational, external, human-made, software, malicious interaction fault (24-25). Heating the RAM with a hairdryer to cause memory errors that permit software security violations would be an external, human-made, hardware, malicious interaction fault (22-23). The vulnerability that an exploit takes advantage of is typically a software flaw (e.g., an unchecked buffer) that could be characterized as a developmental, internal, human-made, software, nonmalicious, nondeliberate, permanent fault (1-2).

3.2.5 On Interaction Faults

Interaction faults occur during the use phase, therefore they are all *operational* faults. They are caused by elements of the use environment (see Section 3.1) interacting with the system; therefore, they are all *external*. Most classes originate due to some human action in the use environment; therefore, they are *human-made*. They are fault classes 16-31 in Fig. 5. An exception are external natural faults (14-15) caused by cosmic rays, solar flares, etc. Here, nature interacts with the system without human participation.

A broad class of human-made operational faults is **configuration faults**, i.e., wrong setting of parameters that can affect security, networking, storage, middleware, etc. [24]. Such faults can occur during configuration changes performed during adaptive or augmentative maintenance performed concurrently with system operation (e.g., introduction of a new software version on a network server); they are then called **reconfiguration faults** [70].

As mentioned in Section 2.2, a common feature of interaction faults is that, in order to be "successful," they usually necessitate the prior presence of a *vulnerability*, i.e., an internal fault that enables an external fault to harm the system. Vulnerabilities can be development or operational faults; they can be malicious or nonmalicious, as

logic bomb: *malicious logic* that remains dormant in the host system till a certain time or an event occurs, or certain conditions are met, and then deletes files, slows down or crashes the host system, etc.

Trojan horse: *malicious logic* performing, or able to perform, an illegitimate action while giving the impression of being legitimate; the illegitimate action can be the disclosure or modification of information (attack against confidentiality or integrity) or a *logic bomb*;

trapdoor: *malicious logic* that provides a means of circumventing access control mechanisms;

virus: *malicious logic* that replicates itself and joins another program when it is executed, thereby turning into a *Trojan horse*; a virus can carry a *logic bomb*;

worm: *malicious logic* that replicates itself and propagates without the users being aware of it; a worm can also carry a *logic bomb*;

zombie: *malicious logic* that can be triggered by an attacker in order to mount a coordinated attack.

Fig. 7. Malicious logic faults.

can be the external faults that exploit them. There are interesting and obvious similarities between an intrusion attempt and a physical external fault that "exploits" a lack of shielding. A vulnerability can result from a deliberate development fault, for economic or for usability reasons, thus resulting in limited protections, or even in their absence.

3.3 Failures

3.3.1 Service Failures
In Section 2.2, a *service failure* is defined as an event that occurs when the delivered service deviates from correct service. The different ways in which the deviation is manifested are a system's *service failure modes*. Each mode can have more than one *service failure severity*.

The occurrence of a failure was defined in Section 2 with respect to the function of a system, not with respect to the description of the function stated in the functional specification: a service delivery complying with the specification may be unacceptable for the system user(s), thus uncovering a specification fault, i.e., revealing the fact that the specification did not adequately describe the system function(s). Such specification faults can be either omission or commission faults (misinterpretations, unwarranted assumptions, inconsistencies, typographical mistakes). In such circumstances, the fact that the event is undesired (and is in fact a failure) may be recognized only after its occurrence, for instance via its consequences. So, failures can be subjective and disputable, i.e., may require judgment to identify and characterize.

The service failure modes characterize incorrect service according to four viewpoints:

1. the failure domain,
2. the detectability of failures,
3. the consistency of failures, and
4. the consequences of failures on the environment.

The **failure domain** viewpoint leads us to distinguish:

- **content failures**. The content of the information delivered at the service interface (i.e., the service content) deviates from implementing the system function.
- **timing failures**. The time of arrival or the duration of the information delivered at the service interface (i.e., the timing of service delivery) deviates from implementing the system function.

These definitions can be specialized: 1) the content can be in numerical or nonnumerical sets (e.g., alphabets, graphics, colors, sounds), and 2) a timing failure may be early or late, depending on whether the service is delivered too **early** or too **late**. Failures when both information and timing are incorrect fall into two classes:

- **halt failure,** or simply **halt,** when the service is _halted_ (the external state becomes constant, i.e., system activity, if there is any, is no longer perceptible to the users); a special case of halt is **silent failure**, or simply **silence**, when no service at all is delivered at the service interface (e.g., no messages are sent in a distributed system).
- **erratic failures** otherwise, i.e., when a service is delivered (not halted), but is _erratic_ (e.g., babbling).

Fig. 8 summarizes the service failure modes with respect to the failure domain viewpoint.

The **detectability** viewpoint addresses the _signaling_ of service failures to the user(s). Signaling at the service interface originates from detecting mechanisms in the system that check the correctness of the delivered service. When the losses are detected and signaled by a warning signal, then **signaled failures** occur. Otherwise, they are **unsignaled failures**. The detecting mechanisms themselves have two failure modes: 1) signaling a loss of function when no failure has actually occurred, that is a **false alarm**, 2) not signaling a function loss, that is an _unsignaled failure_. When the occurrence of service failures result in reduced modes of service, the system signals a degraded mode of service to the user(s). Degraded modes may range from minor reductions to emergency service and safe shutdown.

The consistency of failures leads us to distinguish, when a system has two or more users:

- **consistent failures**. The incorrect service is perceived identically by all system users.
- **inconsistent failures**. Some or all system users perceive differently incorrect service (some users may actually perceive correct service); inconsistent failures are usually called, after [38], **Byzantine failures**.

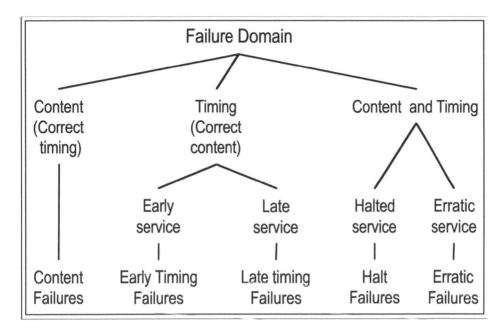

Fig. 8. Service failure modes with respect to the failure domain viewpoint.

Grading the *consequences of the failures* upon the system environment enables failure severities to be defined. The failure modes are ordered into severity levels, to which are generally associated maximum acceptable probabilities of occurrence. The number, the labeling, and the definition of the severity levels, as well as the acceptable probabilities of occurrence, are application-related, and involve the dependability and security attributes for the considered application(s). Examples of criteria for determining the classes of failure severities are

1. for availability, the outage duration;
2. for safety, the possibility of human lives being endangered;
3. for confidentiality, the type of information that may be unduly disclosed; and
4. for integrity, the extent of the corruption of data and the ability to recover from these corruptions.

Generally speaking, two limiting levels can be defined according to the relation between the benefit (in the broad sense of the term, not limited to economic considerations) provided by the service delivered in the absence of failure, and the consequences of failures:

- **minor failures**, where the harmful consequences are of similar cost to the benefits provided by correct service delivery;
- **catastrophic failures**, where the cost of harmful consequences is orders of magnitude, or even incommensurably, higher than the benefit provided by correct service delivery.

Fig. 9 summarizes the service failure modes.

Systems that are designed and implemented so that they fail only in specific modes of failure described in the dependability and security specification and only to an acceptable extent are **fail-controlled systems**, e.g., with stuck output as opposed to delivering erratic values, silence as opposed to babbling, consistent as opposed to inconsistent failures. A system whose failures are to an acceptable extent halting failures only is a **fail-halt** (or fail-stop) **system**; the situations of stuck service and of silence lead, respectively, to **fail-passive systems** and **fail-silent systems** [53]. A system whose failures are, to an acceptable extent, all minor ones is a **fail-safe system**.

As defined in Section 2, delivery of incorrect service is an outage, which lasts until *service restoration*. The outage duration may vary significantly, depending on the actions involved in service restoration after a failure has occurred: 1) automatic or operator-assisted recovery, restart, or reboot; 2) corrective maintenance. Correction of development faults (by patches or workarounds) is usually performed offline, after service restoration, and the upgraded components resulting from fault correction are then introduced at some appropriate time with or without interruption of system operation. Preemptive interruption of system operation for an upgrade or for preventive maintenance is a *service shutdown*, also called a *planned outage* (as opposed to an outage consecutive to failure, which is then called an *unplanned outage*).

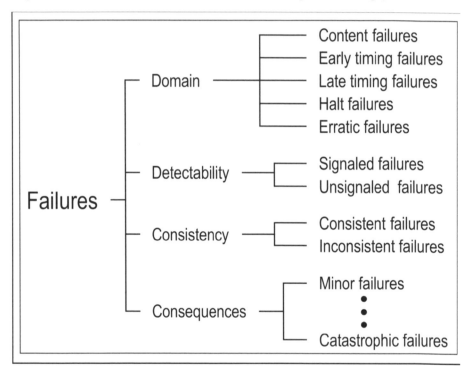

Fig. 9. Service failure modes.

3.3.2 Development Failures

As stated in Section 3.1, development faults may be introduced into the system being developed by its environment, especially by human developers, development tools, and production facilities. Such development faults may contribute to partial or complete development failures, or they may remain undetected until the use phase. A complete **development failure** causes the development process to be terminated before the system is accepted for use and placed into service. There are two aspects of development failures:

1. *Budget failure.* The allocated funds are exhausted before the system passes acceptance testing.
2. *Schedule failure.* The projected delivery schedule slips to a point in the future where the system would be technologically obsolete or functionally inadequate for the user's needs.

The principal causes of development failures are: incomplete or faulty specifications, an excessive number of user-initiated specification changes; inadequate design with respect to functionality and/or performance goals; too many development faults; inadequate fault removal capability; prediction of insufficient dependability or security; and faulty estimates of development costs. All are usually due to an underestimate of the complexity of the system to be developed.

There are two kinds of **partial development failures**, i.e., failures of lesser severity than project termination. Budget or schedule **overruns** occur when the development is completed, but the funds or time needed to complete the effort exceed the original estimates. Another form of partial development failure is **downgrading**: The developed system is delivered with less functionality, lower performance, or is predicted to have lower dependability or security than was required in the original system specification.

Development failures, overruns, and downgrades have a very negative impact on the user community, see, e.g., statistics about large software projects [34], or the analysis of the complete development failure of the AAS system, that resulted in the waste of $1.5 billion [67].

3.3.3 Dependability and Security Failures

It is to be expected that faults of various kinds will affect the system during its use phase. The faults may cause unacceptably degraded performance or total failure to deliver the specified service. For this reason, a dependability and security specification is agreed upon that states the goals for each attribute: availability, reliability, safety, confidentiality, integrity, and maintainability.

The specification explicitly identifies the *classes of faults* that are expected and the use *environment* in which the system will operate. The specification may also require safeguards against certain undesirable or dangerous conditions. Furthermore, the inclusion of specific fault prevention or fault tolerance techniques may be required by the user.

A **dependability or security failure** occurs when the given system suffers service failures more frequently or more severely than acceptable.

The dependability and security specification can also contain faults. Omission faults can occur in description of the use environment or in choice of the classes of faults to be prevented or tolerated. Another class of faults is the unjustified choice of very high requirements for one or more attributes that raises the cost of development and may lead to a cost overrun or even a development failure. For example, the initial AAS complete outage limit of 3 seconds per year was changed to 5 minutes per year for the new contract in 1994 [67].

3.4 Errors

An *error* has been defined in Section 2.2 as the part of a system's total state that may lead to a failure – a failure occurs when the error causes the delivered service to deviate from correct service. The cause of the error has been called a fault.

An error is **detected** if its presence is indicated by an *error message* or *error signal*. Errors that are present but not detected are **latent** errors.

Since a system consists of a set of interacting components, the total state is the set of its component states. The definition implies that a fault originally causes an error within the state of one (or more) components, but service failure will not occur as long as the external state of that component is not part of the external state of the system. Whenever the error becomes a part of the external state of the component, a service failure of that component occurs, but the error remains internal to the entire system.

Whether or not an error will actually lead to a service failure depends on two factors:

1. The structure of the system, and especially the nature of any redundancy that exists in it:

    *   *protective* redundancy, introduced to provide fault tolerance, that is explicitly intended to prevent an error from leading to service failure.
    *   *unintentional* redundancy (it is in practice difficult if not impossible to build a system without any form of redundancy) that may have the same – presumably unexpected – result as intentional redundancy.

2. The behavior of the system: the part of the state that contains an error may never be needed for service, or an error may be eliminated (e.g., when overwritten) before it leads to a failure.

A convenient classification of errors is to describe them in terms of the elementary service failures that they cause, using the terminology of Section 3.3.1: content versus timing errors, detected versus latent errors, consistent versus inconsistent errors when the service goes to two or more users, minor versus catastrophic errors. In the field of error control codes, content errors are further classified according to the damage pattern: single, double, triple, byte, burst, erasure, arithmetic, track, etc., errors.

Some faults (e.g., a burst of electromagnetic radiation) can simultaneously cause errors in more than one component. Such errors are called **multiple related errors**. **Single errors** are errors that affect one component only.

3.5 The Pathology of Failure: Relationship between Faults, Errors, and Failures

The creation and manifestation mechanisms of faults, errors, and failures are illustrated by Fig. 10, and summarized as follows:

1. A fault is *active* when it produces an error; otherwise, it is *dormant*. An active fault is either 1) an internal fault that was previously dormant and that has been activated by the computation process or environmental conditions, or 2) an external fault. **Fault activation** is the application of an input (the activation pattern) to a component that causes a dormant fault to become active. Most internal faults cycle between their dormant and active states.

2. Error propagation within a given component (i.e., *internal* propagation) is caused by the computation process: An error is successively transformed into other errors. Error propagation from component A to component B that receives service from A (i.e., *external* propagation) occurs when, through internal propagation, an error reaches the service interface of component A. At this time, service delivered by A to B becomes incorrect, and the ensuing service failure of A appears as an external fault to B and propagates the error into B via its use interface.

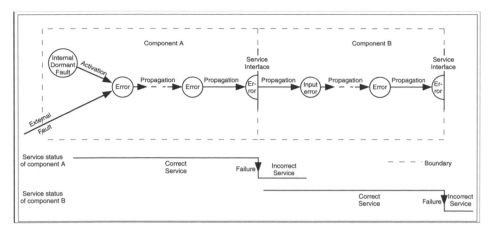

Fig. 10. Error propagation.

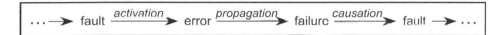

Fig. 11. The fundamental chain of dependability and security threats.

3. A service failure occurs when an error is propagated to the service interface and causes the service delivered by the system to deviate from correct service. The failure of a component causes a permanent or transient fault in the system that contains the component. Service failure of a system causes a permanent or transient external fault for the other system(s) that receive service from the given system.

These mechanisms enable the "chain of threats" to be completed, as indicated by Fig. 11. The arrows in this chain express a causality relationship between faults, errors, and failures. They should be interpreted generically: by propagation, several errors can be generated before a failure occurs. It is worth emphasizing that, from the mechanisms above listed, propagation, and, thus, instantiation(s) of this chain, can occur via interaction between components or systems, composition of components into a system, and the creation or modification of a system.

Some illustrative examples of fault pathology are given in Fig. 12. From those examples, it is easily understood that fault dormancy may vary considerably, depending upon the fault, the given system's utilization, etc.

The ability to identify the activation pattern of a fault that had caused one or more errors is the **fault activation reproducibility**. Faults can be categorized according to their activation reproducibility: Faults whose activation is reproducible are called solid, or hard, faults, whereas faults whose activation is not systematically reproducible are elusive, or soft, faults. Most residual development faults in large and complex software are elusive faults: They are intricate enough that their activation conditions depend on complex combinations of internal state and external requests, that occur rarely and can be very difficult to reproduce [23]. Other examples of elusive faults are:

- "pattern sensitive" faults in semiconductor memories, changes in the parameters of a hardware component (effects of temperature variation, delay in timing due to parasitic capacitance, etc.).

- A short circuit occurring in an integrated circuit is a *failure* (with respect to the function of the circuit); the consequence (connection stuck at a Boolean value, modification of the circuit function, etc.) is a *fault* that will remain dormant as long as it is not activated. Upon activation (invoking the faulty component and uncovering the fault by an appropriate input pattern), the fault becomes *active* and produces an *error*, which is likely to propagate and create other errors. If and when the propagated error(s) affect(s) the delivered service (in information content and/or in the timing of delivery), a *failure* occurs.

- The result of an *error* by a programmer leads to a *failure* to write the correct instruction or data, that in turn results in a *(dormant) fault* in the written software (faulty instruction(s) or data); upon activation (invoking the component where the fault resides and triggering the faulty instruction, instruction sequence or data by an appropriate input pattern) the fault becomes *active* and produces an *error*; if and when the error affects the delivered service (in information content and/or in the timing of delivery), a *failure* occurs. This example is not restricted to accidental faults: a *logic bomb* is created by a malicious programmer; it will remain *dormant* until activated (e.g. at some predetermined date); it then produces an *error* that may lead to a storage overflow or to slowing down the program execution; as a consequence, service delivery will suffer from a so-called *denial-of-service*.

- The result of an *error* by a specifier leads to a *failure* to describe a function, that in turn results in a *fault* in the written specification, e.g. incomplete description of the function. The implemented system therefore does not incorporate the missing (sub-)function. When the input data are such that the service corresponding to the missing function should be delivered, the actual service delivered will be different from expected service, i.e., an *error* will be perceived by the user, and a *failure* will thus occur.

- An inappropriate human-system interaction performed by an operator during the operation of the system is an external *fault* (from the system viewpoint); the resulting altered processed data is an *error*; etc.

- An *error* in reasoning leads to a maintenance or operating manual writer's *failure* to write correct directives, that in turn results in a *fault* in the corresponding manual (faulty directives) that will remain *dormant* as long as the directives are not acted upon in order to address a given situation, etc.

- A failure often results from the combined action of several faults; this is especially true when considering security issues: a trap-door (i.e., some way to by-pass access control) that is inserted into a computing system, either accidentally or deliberately, is a development *fault*; this fault may remain *dormant* until some malicious human makes use of it to enter the system; the intruder login is a deliberate interaction *fault*; when the intruder is logged in, he or she may deliberately create an *error*, e.g., modifying some file (integrity attack); when this file is used by an authorized user, the service will be affected, and a *failure* will occur.

- A given fault in a given component may result from various different possible sources; for instance, a permanent *fault* in a physical component — e.g., stuck at ground voltage — may result from:
- a physical *failure* (e.g., caused by a threshold change),
- an *error* caused by a development *fault* — e.g., faulty microinstruction decoding circuitry propagating 'down' through the layers and causing an illegal short between two circuit outputs for a duration long enough to provoke a short-circuit having the same consequence as a threshold change.

- Another example of top-down propagation is the exploitation during operation of an inadvertently introduced buffer overflow for gaining root privilege and subsequently re-writing the flash-ROM.

Fig. 12. Examples illustrating fault pathology.

- conditions – affecting either hardware or software – that occur when the system load exceeds a certain level, causing, for example, marginal timing and synchronization.

The similarity of the manifestation of elusive development faults and of transient physical faults leads to both classes being grouped together as **intermittent faults**. Errors produced by intermittent faults are usually termed **soft errors**. Fig. 13. summarizes this discussion.

Situations involving multiple faults and/or failures are frequently encountered. System failures often turn out on later examination to have been caused by errors that are due to a number of different coexisting faults. Given a system with defined boundaries, a **single fault** is a fault caused by *one* adverse physical event or one harmful human action. **Multiple faults** are *two or more* concurrent, overlapping, or sequential single faults whose consequences, i.e., errors, overlap in time, that is, the errors due to these faults are concurrently present in the system. Consideration of multiple faults leads one to distinguish 1) **independent faults**, that are attributed to different causes, and 2) **related faults**, that are attributed to a common cause. Related faults generally cause *similar errors*, i.e., errors that cannot be distinguished by whatever detection mechanisms are being employed, whereas independent faults usually cause *distinct errors*. However, it may happen that independent faults (especially omissions) lead to similar errors [6], or that related faults lead to distinct errors. The failures caused by similar errors are **common-mode failures**.

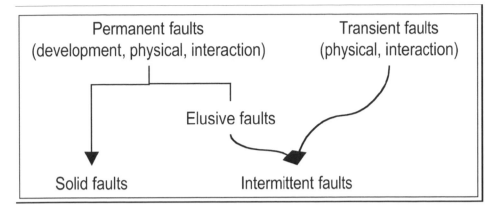

Fig. 13. Solid versus intermittent faults.

Three additional comments, about the words, or labels, "threats," "fault," "error," and "failure:"

1. The use of *threats*, for generically referring to faults, errors, and failures has a broader meaning than its common use in security, where it essentially retains it usual notion of potentiality. In our terminology, it has both this potentiality aspect (e.g., faults being not yet active, service failures not having impaired dependability), and a realization aspect (e.g., active fault, error that is present, service failure that occurs). In security terms, a malicious external fault is an *attack*.

2. The exclusive use in this paper of faults, errors, and failures does not preclude the use in special situations of words which designate, briefly and unambiguously, a specific class of threat; this is especially applicable to faults (e.g., bug, defect, deficiency, flaw, erratum) and to failures (e.g., breakdown, malfunction, denial-of-service).

3. The assignment made of the particular terms fault, error, and failure simply takes into account common usage: 1) fault prevention, tolerance, and diagnosis, 2) error detection and correction, 3) failure rate.

4. Dependability, Security, and their Attributes

4.1 The Definitions of Dependability and Security

In Section 2.3, we have presented two alternate definitions of dependability:

*   the original definition: the ability to deliver service that can justifiably be trusted.
*   an alternate definition: the ability of a system to avoid service failures that are more frequent or more severe than is acceptable.

The original definition is a general definition that aims to generalize the more classical notions of availability, reliability, safety, integrity, maintainability, etc., that then become attributes of dependability. The alternate definition of dependability comes from the following argument. A system can, and usually does, fail. Is it however still dependable? When does it become undependable? The alternate definition thus provides a criterion for deciding whether or not, in spite of service failures, a system is still to be regarded as dependable. In addition, the notion of dependability failure, that is directly deduced from that definition, enables the establishment of a connection with development failures.

The definitions of dependability that exist in current standards differ from our definitions. Two such differing definitions are:

- "The collective term used to describe the availability performance and its influencing factors: reliability performance, maintainability performance and maintenance support performance" [31].

- "The extent to which the system can be relied upon to perform exclusively and correctly the system task(s) under defined operational and environmental conditions over a defined period of time, or at a given instant of time" [29].

The ISO definition is clearly centered upon availability. This is no surprise as this definition can be traced back to the definition given by the international organization for telephony, the CCITT [11], at a time when availability was the main concern to telephone operating companies. However, the willingness to grant dependability a generic character is noteworthy, since it goes beyond availability as it was usually defined, and relates it to reliability and maintainability. In this respect, the ISO/CCITT definition is consistent with the definition given in [26] for dependability: "the probability that a system will operate when needed." The second definition, from [29], introduces the notion of reliance, and as such is much closer to our definitions.

Terminology in the security world has its own rich history. Computer security, communications security, information security, and information assurance are terms that have had a long development and use in the community of security researchers and practitioners, mostly without direct reference to dependability. Nevertheless, all of these terms can be understood in terms of the three primary security attributes of confidentiality, integrity, and availability.

Security has not been characterized as a single attribute of dependability. This is in agreement with the usual definitions of security, that view it as a *composite* notion, namely, "the combination of confidentiality, the prevention of the unauthorized disclosure of information, integrity, the prevention of the unauthorized amendment or deletion of information, and availability, the prevention of the unauthorized withholding of information" [12], [52]. Our unified definition for **security** is the absence of unauthorized access to, or handling of, system state. The relationship between dependability and security is illustrated by Fig. 14, that is a refinement of Fig. 1.

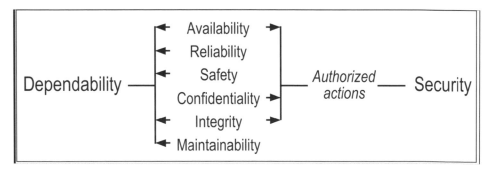

Fig. 14. Relationship between dependability and security.

4.2 Dependence and Trust

We have introduced the notions of dependence and trust in Section 2.3:

- The dependence of system A on system B represents the extent to which System A's dependability is (or would be) affected by that of System B.
- Trust is accepted dependence.

The dependence of a system on another system can vary from total dependence (any failure of B would cause A to fail) to complete independence (B cannot cause A to fail). If there is reason to believe that B's dependability will be insufficient for A's required dependability, the former should be enhanced, A's dependence reduced, or additional means of fault tolerance provided. Our definition of dependence relates to the relation *depends upon* [50], [14], whose definition is a component a depends upon a component *b* if the correctness of *b*'s service delivery is necessary for the correctness of *a*'s service delivery. However, this relation is expressed in terms of the narrower concept of correctness, rather than dependability, and, hence, is only binary, whereas our notion of dependence can take values on a measurable space.

By accepted dependence, we mean the dependence (say of A on B) allied to a judgment that this level of dependence is acceptable. Such a judgment (made by or on behalf of A) about B is possibly explicit and even laid down in a contract between A and B, but might be only implicit, even unthinking. Indeed, it might even be unwilling – in that A has no alternative option but to put its trust in B. Thus, to the extent that A trusts B, it need not assume responsibility for, i.e., provide means of tolerating, B's failures (the question of whether it is capable of doing this is another matter). In fact, the extent to which A fails to provide means of tolerating B's failures is a measure of A's (perhaps unthinking or unwilling) trust in B.

4.3. The Attributes of Dependability and Security

The attributes of dependability and security that have been defined in Section 2.3 may be of varying importance depending on the application intended for the given computing system: Availability, integrity, and maintainability are generally required, although to a varying degree depending on the application, whereas reliability, safety, and confidentiality may or may not be required according to the application. The extent to which a system possesses the attributes of dependability and security should be considered in a relative, probabilistic, sense, and not in an absolute, deterministic sense: Due to the unavoidable presence or occurrence of faults, systems are never totally available, reliable, safe, or secure.

The definition given for integrity – absence of improper system state alterations – goes beyond the usual definitions, that 1) relate to the notion of authorized actions only, and 2) focus on information (e.g., prevention of the unauthorized amendment or deletion of information [12], assurance of approved data alterations [33]): 1) naturally, when a system implements an authorization policy, "improper" encompasses "unauthorized," 2) "improper alterations" encompass actions that prevent (correct) upgrades of information, and 3) "system state" includes system modifications or damages.

The definition given for maintainability intentionally goes beyond corrective and preventive maintenance, and encompasses the other forms of maintenance defined in Section 3, i.e., adaptive and augmentative maintenance. The concept of **autonomic computing** [22] has as its major aim the provision of high maintainability for large networked computer systems, though automation of their management.

Besides the attributes defined in Section 2 and discussed above, other, *secondary*, attributes can be defined, which refine or specialize the *primary* attributes as defined in Section 2. An example of a specialized secondary attribute is robustness, i.e., dependability with respect to external faults, which characterizes a system reaction to a specific class of faults.

The notion of secondary attributes is especially relevant for security, and is based on distinguishing among various types of information [9]. Examples of such secondary attributes are:

- **accountability**: availability and integrity of the identity of the person who performed an operation;
- **authenticity**: integrity of a message content and origin, and possibly of some other information, such as the time of emission;

nonrepudiability: availability and ë of security-motivated constraints, that are to be adhered to by, for example, an organization or a computer system [47]. The enforcement of such constraints may be via technical, management, and/or operational controls, and the policy may lay down how these controls are to be enforced. In effect, therefore, a security policy is a (partial) system specification, lack of adherence to which will be regarded as a security failure. In practice, there may be a hierarchy of such security policies, relating to a hierarchy of systems – for example, an entire company, its information systems department, and the individuals and computer systems in this department. Separate, albeit related policies, or separate parts of an overall policy document, may be created concerning different security issues, e.g., a policy regarding the controlled public disclosure of company information, one on physical and networked access to the company's computers. Some computer security policies include constraints on how information may flow within a system as well as constraints on system states.

As with any set of dependability and security specifications, issues of completeness, consistency, and accuracy are of great importance. There has thus been extensive research on methods for formally expressing and analyzing security policies. However, if some system activity is found to be in a contravention of a relevant security policy then, as with any system specification, the security failure may either be that of the system, or because the policy does not adequately describe the intended security requirement. A well-known example of an apparently satisfactory security policy that proved to be deficient, by failing to specify some particular behavior as insecure, is discussed by [44].

Dependability and security classes are generally defined via the analysis of failure frequencies and severities, and of outage durations, for the attributes that are of concern for a given application. This analysis may be conducted directly or indirectly via risk assessment (see, e.g., [25] for availability, [58] for safety, and [32] for security).

The variations in the emphasis placed on the different attributes directly influence the balance of the techniques (fault prevention, tolerance, removal, and forecasting) to be employed in order to make the resulting system dependable and secure. This problem is all the more difficult as some of the attributes are conflicting (e.g., availability and safety, availability and confidentiality), necessitating that trade offs be made.

4.4 Dependability, High Confidence, Survivability, and Trustworthiness

Other concepts similar to dependability exist, such as **high confidence, survivability**, and **trustworthiness.** They are presented and compared to dependability in Fig. 15. A sideby- side comparison leads to the conclusion that all four concepts are essentially equivalent in their goals and address similar threats.

Concept	Dependability	High Confidence	Survivability	Trustworthiness
Goal	1) ability to deliver service that can justifiably be trusted 2) ability of a system to avoid service failures that are more frequent or more severe than is acceptable	consequences of the system behavior are well understood and predictable	capability of a system to fulfill its mission in a timely manner	assurance that a system will perform as expected
Threats present	1) development faults (e.g., software flaws, hardware errata, malicious logic) 2) physical faults (e.g., production defects, physical deterioration) 3) interaction faults (e.g., physical interference, input mistakes, attacks, including viruses, worms, intrusions)	• internal and external threats • naturally occurring hazards and malicious attacks from a sophisticated and well-funded adversary	1) attacks (e.g., intrusions, probes, denials of service) 2) failures (internally generated events due to, e.g., software design errors, hardware degradation, human errors, corrupted data) 3) accidents (externally generated events such as natural disasters)	1) hostile attacks (from hackers or insiders) 2) environmental disruptions (accidental disruptions, either man-made or natural) 3) human and operator errors (e.g., software flaws, mistakes by human operators)
Reference	This paper	"Information Technology Frontiers for a New Millennium (Blue Book 2000)" [48]	"Survivable network systems" [16]	"Trust in cyberspace" [62]

Fig. 15. Dependability, high confidence, survivability, and trustworthiness.

5. The Means to Attain Dependability and Security

In this section, we examine in turn fault prevention, fault tolerance, fault removal, and fault forecasting. The section ends with a discussion on the relationship between these various means.

5.1. Fault Prevention

Fault prevention is part of general engineering, and, as such, will not be much emphasized here. However, there are facets of fault prevention that are of direct interest regarding dependability and security, and that can be discussed according to the classes of faults defined in Section 3.2.

Prevention of development faults is an obvious aim for development methodologies, both for software (e.g., information hiding, modularization, and use of strongly-typed programming languages) and hardware (e.g., design rules). Improvement of development processes in order to reduce the number of faults introduced in the produced systems is a step further in that it is based on the recording of faults in the products, and the elimination of the causes of the faults via process modifications [13], [51].

5.2. Fault Tolerance

5.2.1. Fault Tolerance Techniques

Fault tolerance [3], which is aimed at failure avoidance, is carried out via error detection and system recovery. Fig. 16 gives the techniques involved in fault tolerance.

Usually, fault handling is followed by corrective maintenance, aimed at removing faults that were isolated by fault handling; in other words, the factor that distinguishes fault tolerance from maintenance is that maintenance requires the participation of an external agent. Closed systems are those systems where fault removal cannot be practically implemented (e.g., the hardware of a deep space probe).

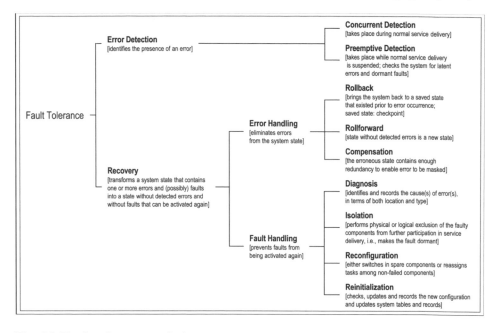

Fig. 16. Fault tolerance techniques.

Rollback and rollforward are invoked on demand, after error detection has taken place, whereas compensation can be applied either on demand or systematically, at predetermined times or events, independently of the presence or absence of (detected) error. Error handling on demand followed by fault handling together form system recovery; hence, the name of the corresponding strategy for fault tolerance: **error detection and system recovery** or simply **detection and recovery**.

Fault masking, or simply **masking**, results from the systematic usage of compensation. Such masking will conceal a possibly progressive and eventually fatal loss of protective redundancy. So, practical implementations of masking generally involve error detection (and possibly fault handling), leading to **masking and recovery**.

It is noteworthy that:

1. Rollback and roll forward are not mutually exclusive. Rollback may be attempted first; if the error persists, roll forward may then be attempted.

2. Intermittent faults do not necessitate isolation or reconfiguration; identifying whether a fault is intermittent or not can be performed either by error

handling (error recurrence indicates that the fault is not intermittent), or via fault diagnosis when roll forward is used.

3. Fault handling may directly follow error detection, without error handling being attempted.

Preemptive error detection and handling, possibly followed by fault handling, is commonly performed at system power up. It also comes into play during operation, under various forms such as spare checking, memory scrubbing, audit programs, or so-called **software rejuvenation** [27], aimed at removing the effects of software aging before they lead to failure. Fig. 17 gives four typical and schematic examples for the various strategies identified for implementing fault tolerance.

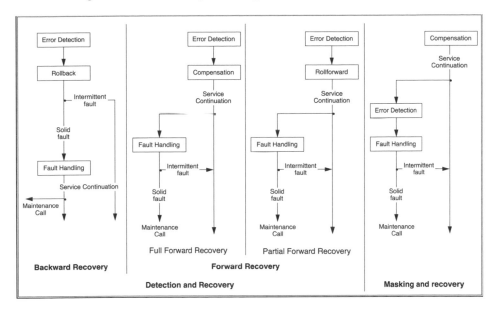

Fig. 17. Examples for the basic strategies for implementing fault tolerance.

5.2.2. Implementation of Fault Tolerance

The choice of error detection, error handling and fault handling techniques, and of their implementation is directly related to and strongly dependent upon the underlying fault assumption: The class(es) of faults that can actually be tolerated depend(s) on the fault assumption that is being considered in the development process and, thus, relies on the *independence* of redundancies with respect to the process of fault creation and activation. A (widely used) method of achieving fault tolerance is to perform multiple computations through multiple channels, either sequentially or concurrently. When tolerance of physical faults is foreseen, the channels may be of identical design, based on the assumption that hardware components fail independently. Such an approach has proven to be adequate for elusive development faults, via rollback [23], [28]; it is however not suitable for the tolerance of solid development faults, which necessitates that the channels implement the same function via separate designs and implementations [57], [4], i.e., through **design diversity** [6].

The provision within a component of the required functional processing capability together with concurrent error detection mechanisms leads to the notion of self-checking component, either in hardware or in software; one of the important benefits of the **self-checking component** approach is the ability to give a clear definition of *error confinement areas* [63].

It is evident that not all fault tolerance techniques are equally effective. The measure of effectiveness of any given fault tolerance technique is called its **coverage**. The imperfections of fault tolerance, i.e., the lack of *fault tolerance coverage*, constitute a severe limitation to the increase in dependability that can be obtained. Such imperfections of fault tolerance (Fig. 18) are due either

1.   to development faults affecting the fault tolerance mechanisms with respect to the fault assumptions stated during the development, the consequence of which is a lack of *error and fault handling coverage* (defined with respect to a class of errors or faults, e.g., single errors, stuck-at faults, etc., as the conditional probability that the technique is effective, given that the errors or faults have occurred), or

2.   to fault assumptions that differ from the faults really occurring in operation, resulting in a lack of *fault assumption coverage*, that can be in turn due to either 1) failed component(s) not behaving as assumed, that is a lack of *failure mode coverage*, or 2) the occurrence of common-mode failures when independent ones are assumed, that is a lack of *failure independence coverage*.

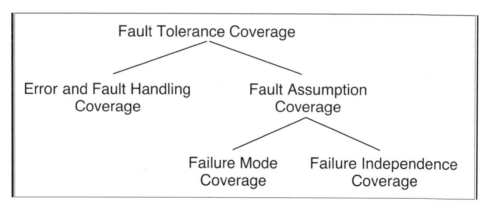

Fig. 18. Fault tolerance coverage.

The lack of error and fault handling coverage has been shown to be a drastic limit to dependability improvement [8], [1]. Similar effects can result from the lack of failure mode coverage: conservative fault assumptions (e.g., Byzantine faults) will result in a higher failure mode coverage, at the expense of necessitating an increase in the redundancy and more complex fault tolerance mechanisms, which can lead to an overall decrease in system dependability and security [54].

An important issue in coordination of the activities of multiple components is prevention of error propagation from affecting the operation of no failed components. This issue becomes particularly important when a given component needs to communicate some information to other components. Typical examples of such *single-source information* are local sensor data, the value of a local clock, the local view of the status of other components, etc. The consequence of this need to communicate single-source information from one component to other components is that no failed components must reach an agreement as to how the information they obtain should be employed in a mutually consistent way. This is known as the *consensus* problem [43].

Fault tolerance is (also) a recursive concept: it is essential that the mechanisms that implement fault tolerance should be protected against the faults that might affect them. Examples of such protection are voter replication, self checking checkers, "stable" memory for recovery programs and data.

Systematic introduction of fault tolerance is often facilitated by the addition of support systems specialized for fault tolerance (e.g., software monitors, service processors, and dedicated communication links).

Reflection, a technique for transparently and appropriately augmenting all relevant actions of an object or software component, e.g., in order to ensure that these actions can be undone if necessary, can be used in object-oriented software and through the provision of middleware [17].

Fault tolerance applies to all classes of faults. Protection against intrusions traditionally involves cryptography and firewalls. Some mechanisms of error detection are directed towards both no malicious and malicious faults (e.g., memory access protection techniques). Intrusion detection is usually performed via likelihood checks [18], [15].

Approaches and schemes have been proposed for tolerating:

- intrusions and physical faults, via information fragmentation and dispersal [20], [56],
- malicious logic, and more specifically to viruses, either via control flow checking [35], or via design diversity [36],
- intrusions, malicious logic, vulnerabilities due to physical or development faults, via server diversity [68].

Finally, it is worth mentioning that 1) several synonyms exist for fault tolerance: **self-repair, self-healing, resilience**, and that 2) the term **recovery-oriented computing** [19] has recently been introduced for what is essentially a fault tolerance approach to achieving overall system dependability, i.e., at the level above individual computer systems, in which the failures of these individual systems constitute the faults to be tolerated.

5.3. Fault Removal

In this section, we consider fault removal during system development, and during system use.

5.3.1. Fault Removal During Development

Fault removal during *the development phase* of a system lifecycle consists of three steps: **verification**, diagnosis, and correction. We focus in what follows on verification that is the process of checking whether the system adheres to given properties, termed the **verification conditions**; if it does not, the other two steps have to be undertaken: diagnosing the fault(s) that prevented the verification conditions from being fulfilled, and then performing the necessary corrections. After correction, the verification process should be repeated in order to check that fault removal had no undesired consequences; the verification performed at this stage is usually termed **no regression verification**.

Checking the specification is usually referred to as **validation** [7]. Uncovering specification faults can happen at any stage of the development, either during the specification phase itself, or during subsequent phases when evidence is found that the system will not implement its function, or that the implementation cannot be achieved in a cost-effective way.

Verification techniques can be classified according to whether or not they involve exercising the system. Verifying a system without actual execution is **static verification**. Such verification can be conducted:

- on the system itself, in the form of 1) *static analysis* (e.g., inspections or walk-through, data flow analysis, complexity analysis, abstract interpretation, compiler checks, vulnerability search, etc.) or 2) *theorem proving*;
- on a model of the system behavior, where the model is usually a state-transition model (Petri nets, finite or infinite state automata), leading to *model checking*.

Verifying a system through exercising it constitutes **dynamic verification**; the inputs supplied to the system can be either symbolic in the case of **symbolic execution**, or actual in the case of verification testing, usually simply termed **testing**.

Fig. 19 summarizes the verification approaches.

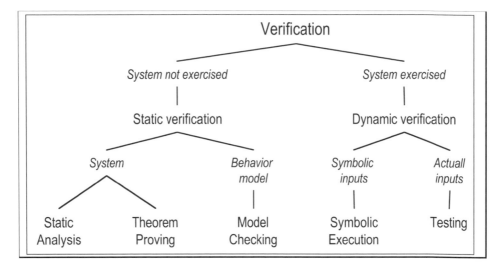

Fig. 19. Verification approaches.

Exhaustive testing of a system with respect to all its possible inputs is generally impractical. The methods for the determination of the test patterns can be classified according to two viewpoints: criteria for selecting the test inputs, and generation of the test inputs.

Fig. 20 summarizes the various testing approaches according to test selection. The upper part of the figure identifies the elementary testing approaches. The lower part of the figure gives the combination of the elementary approaches, where a distinction is made between hardware and software testing since hardware testing is mainly aimed at removing production faults, whereas software testing is concerned only with development faults: hardware testing is usually fault-based, whereas software testing is criteria-based, with the exception of mutation testing, which is fault-based.

The *generation* of the test inputs may be deterministic or probabilistic:

- In **deterministic testing**, test patterns are predetermined by a selective choice.
- In **random**, or **statistical, testing**, test patterns are selected according to a defined probability distribution on the input domain; the distribution and the number of input data are determined according to the given fault model or criteria.

Observing the test outputs and deciding whether or not they satisfy the verification conditions is known as the **oracle problem**. The verification conditions may apply to the whole set of outputs or to a compact function of the latter (e.g., a system signature when testing for physical faults in hardware, or to a "partial oracle" when testing for development faults of software [69]). When testing for physical faults, the results—compact or not—anticipated from the system under test for a given input sequence are determined by simulation or from a reference system (**golden unit**). For development faults, the reference is generally the specification; it may also be a prototype, or another implementation of the same specification in the case of design diversity (**back-to-back testing**).

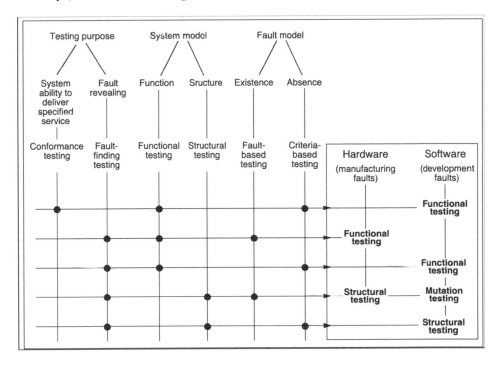

Fig. 20. Testing approaches according to test pattern selection.

Verification methods can be used in combination. For instance, symbolic execution may be used to facilitate the determination of the testing patterns, theorem proving may be used to check properties of infinite state models [60], and mutation testing may be used to compare various testing strategies [66].

As verification has to be performed throughout a system's development, the above techniques are applicable to the various forms taken by a system during its development: prototype, component, etc.

The above techniques apply also to the verification of fault tolerance mechanisms, especially 1) formal static verification [59], and 2) testing that necessitates faults or errors to be part of the test patterns, that is usually referred to as **fault injection** [2].

Verifying that the system *cannot do more* than what is specified is especially important with respect to what the system should not do, thus with respect to safety and security (e.g., **penetration testing**).

Designing a system in order to facilitate its verification is termed **design for verifiability**. This approach is well developed for hardware with respect to physical faults, where the corresponding techniques are termed **design for testability.**

5.3.2. Fault Removal During Use

Fault removal during the use of a system is corrective or preventive maintenance. Corrective maintenance aims to remove faults that have produced one or more errors and have been reported, while preventive maintenance is aimed at uncovering and removing faults before they might cause errors during normal operation. The latter faults include 1) physical faults that have occurred since the last preventive maintenance actions, and 2) development faults that have led to errors in other similar systems. Corrective maintenance for development faults is usually performed in stages: The fault may be first isolated (e.g., by a workaround or a patch) before the actual removal is completed. These forms of maintenance apply to nonfault-tolerant systems as well as to fault-tolerant systems, that can be maintainable online (without interrupting service delivery) or offline (during service outage).

5.4. Fault Forecasting

Fault forecasting is conducted by performing an *evaluation of the system behavior* with respect to fault occurrence or activation. Evaluation has two aspects:

- **qualitative**, or **ordinal, evaluation**, that aims to identify, classify, and rank the failure modes, or the event combinations (component failures or environmental conditions) that would lead to system failures;
- **quantitative**, or **probabilistic, evaluation**, that aims to evaluate in terms of probabilities the extent to which some of the attributes are satisfied; those attributes are then viewed as *measures*.

The methods for qualitative and quantitative evaluation are either specific (e.g., failure mode and effect analysis for qualitative evaluation, or Markov chains and stochastic Petri nets for quantitative evaluation), or they can be used to perform both forms of evaluation (e.g., reliability block diagrams, fault-trees).

The two main approaches to probabilistic fault-forecasting, aimed to derive probabilistic estimates, are *modeling* and *(evaluation) testing*. These approaches are complementary since modeling needs data on the basic processes modeled (failure process, maintenance process, system activation process, etc.), that may be obtained either by testing, or by the processing of failure data.

Modeling can be conducted with respect to 1) physical faults, 2) development faults, or 3) a combination of both. Although modeling is usually performed with respect to no malicious faults, attempts to perform modeling with respect to malicious faults are worth mentioning [49], [61].

Modeling is composed of two phases:

- The *construction* of a model of the system from the elementary stochastic processes that model the behavior of the components of the system and their interactions; these elementary stochastic processes relate to failure, to service restoration including repair, and possibly to system duty cycle or phases of activity.

▪ *Processing* the model to obtain the expressions and the values of the dependability measures of the system.

Generally, several services can be distinguished, as well as two or more modes of service, e.g., ranging from full capacity to emergency service. These modes distinguish less and less complete service deliveries. Performance-related measures of dependability are usually subsumed into the notion of performability [45], [64].

Reliability growth models, either for hardware, for software, or for both, are used to perform reliability predictions from data about past system failures.

Evaluation testing can be characterized using the viewpoints defined in Section 5.3.1, i.e., conformance, functional, non-fault-based, statistical, testing, although it is not— primarily—aimed at verifying a system. A major concern is that the input profile should be representative of the operational profile [46]; hence, the usual name of evaluation testing is **operational testing.**

When evaluating fault-tolerant systems, the coverage provided by error and fault handling mechanisms has a drastic influence [8], [1] on dependability measures. The evaluation of coverage can be performed either through modeling or through testing, i.e., *fault injection.*

The notion of **dependability and security benchmark**, that is a procedure to assess measures of the behavior of a computer system in the presence of faults, enables the integration of the various techniques of fault forecasting in a unified framework. Such a benchmark enables 1) *characterization* of the dependability and security of a system, and 2) *comparison* of alternative or competitive solutions according to one or several attributes [37].

5.5. Relationships between the Means for Dependability and Security

All the "how to's" that appear in the definitions of fault prevention, fault tolerance, fault removal, fault forecasting given in Section 2 are in fact goals that can rarely if ever be fully reached since all the design and analysis activities are human activities, and thus imperfect. These imperfections bring in *relationships* that explain why it is only the *combined* utilization of the above activities—preferably at each step of the design and implementation process—that can best lead to a dependable and secure computing system. These relationships can be sketched as follows: In spite of fault prevention by means of development methodologies and construction rules (themselves imperfect in order to be workable), faults may occur. Hence, there is a need for fault removal. Fault removal is itself imperfect (i.e., all faults cannot be found, and another fault(s) may be introduced when removing a fault), and off-the-shelf components —hardware or software—of the system may, and usually do, contain faults; hence the importance of fault forecasting (besides the analysis of the likely consequences of operational faults). Our increasing dependence on computing systems brings in the requirement for fault tolerance that is in turn based on construction rules; hence, the need again for applying fault removal and fault forecasting to fault tolerance mechanisms themselves. It must be noted that the process is even more recursive than it appears above: Current computing systems are so complex that their design and implementation need software and hardware tools in order to be cost-effective (in a broad sense, including the capability of succeeding within an acceptable time scale). These tools themselves have to be dependable and secure, and so on.

The preceding reasoning illustrates the close interactions between fault removal and fault forecasting, and motivates their gathering into **dependability and security analysis,** aimed at *reaching confidence* in the ability to deliver a service that can be trusted, whereas the grouping of fault prevention and fault tolerance constitutes **dependability and security provision**, aimed at *providing* the ability to deliver a service that can be trusted. Another grouping of the means is the association of 1) fault prevention and fault removal into **fault avoidance**, i.e., how to *aim for* fault-free systems, and of 2) fault tolerance and fault forecasting into **fault acceptance**, i.e., how to *live with* systems that are subject to faults. Fig. 21 illustrates the groupings of the means for dependability. It is noteworthy that, when focusing on security, such analysis is called *security evaluation* [32].

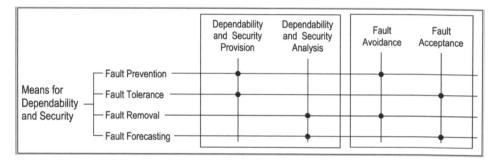

Fig. 21. Groupings of the means for dependability and security.

Besides highlighting the need to assess the procedures and mechanisms of fault tolerance, the consideration of fault removal and fault forecasting as two constituents of the same activity – dependability analysis – leads to a better understanding of the notion of coverage and, thus, of an important problem introduced by the above recursion: *the assessment of the assessment*, or how to reach confidence in the methods and tools used in building confidence in the system. **Coverage** refers here to a measure of the representativeness of the situations to which the system is subjected during its analysis compared to the actual situations that the system will be confronted with during its operational life. The notion of coverage as defined here is very general; it may be made more precise by indicating its range of application, e.g., coverage of a software test with respect to the software text, control graph, etc., coverage of an integrated circuit test with respect to a fault model, coverage of fault tolerance with respect to a class of faults, coverage of a development assumption with respect to reality.

The *assessment* of whether a system is truly dependable and, if appropriate, secure – i.e., the delivered service can justifiably be trusted – goes beyond the analysis techniques as they have been addressed in the previous sections for, at least, the three following reasons and limitations:

■   Precise checking of the coverage of the design or validation assumptions with respect to reality (e.g., relevance to actual faults of the criteria used for determining test inputs, fault hypotheses in the design of fault tolerance mechanisms) would imply a knowledge and a mastering of the technology used, of the intended utilization of the system, etc., that exceeds by far what is generally achievable.

- The evaluation of a system for some attributes of dependability, and especially of security with respect to certain classes of faults is currently considered as unfeasible or as yielding no significant results because probability-theoretic bases do not exist or are not yet widely accepted; examples are safety with respect to accidental development faults, security with respect to intentional faults.

- The specifications with respect to which analysis is performed are likely to contain faults – as does any system.

  Among the numerous consequences of this state of affairs, let us mention:

- The emphasis placed on the development process when assessing a system, i.e., on the methods and techniques utilized in development and how they are employed; in some cases, a *grade* is assigned and delivered to the system according to 1) the nature of the methods and techniques employed in development, and 2) an assessment of their utilization [51], [58], [32], [65].

- The presence, in the specifications of some fault tolerant systems (in addition to probabilistic requirements in terms of dependability measures), of a list of types and numbers of faults that are to be tolerated; such a specification would not be necessary if the limitations mentioned above could be overcome (such specifications are classical in aerospace applications, under the form of a concatenation of "fail-operational" (FO) or "fail-safe" (FS) requirements, e.g., FO/FS, or FO/FO/FS, etc.).

6. Conclusion

Increasingly, individuals and organizations are developing or procuring sophisticated computing systems on whose services they need to place great trust – whether to service a set of cash dispensers, control a satellite constellation, an airplane, a nuclear plant, or a radiation therapy device, or to maintain the confidentiality of a sensitive data base. In differing circumstances, the focus will be on differing properties of such services – e.g., on the average real-time response achieved, the likelihood of producing the required results, the ability to avoid failures that could be catastrophic to the system's environment, or the degree to which deliberate intrusions can be prevented. Simultaneous consideration of dependability and security provides a very convenient means of subsuming these various concerns within a single conceptual framework. It includes as special cases such properties as availability, reliability, safety, confidentiality, integrity, maintainability. It also provides the means of addressing the problem that what a user usually needs from a system is an *appropriate balance* of these properties.

A major strength of the concept formulated in this paper, is its integrative nature; this enables the more classical notions of reliability, availability, safety, confidentiality, integrity, and maintainability to be put into perspective. The fault-error-failure model is central to the understanding and mastering of the various threats that may affect a system, and it enables a unified presentation of these threats, while preserving their specificities via the various fault classes that can be defined. The model provided for the means for achieving dependability and security is extremely useful, as those means are much more orthogonal to each other than the more classical classification according to the attributes of dependability, with respect to which the development of any real system has to perform trade offs since these attributes tend to conflict with each other. The refinement of the basic definitions given in Section 2 leads to a refined dependability and security tree, as given by Fig. 22.

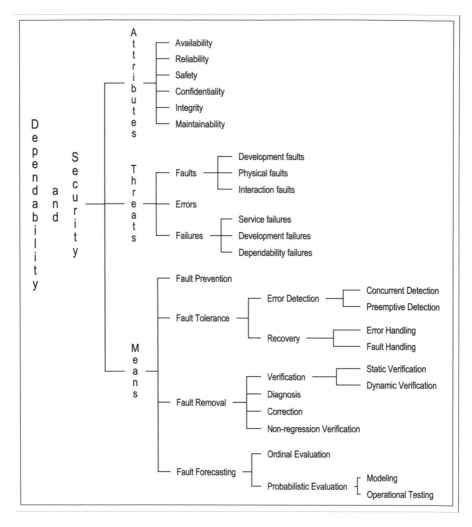

Fig. 22. A refined dependability and security tree.

Appendix

Index of Definitions

Acknowledgments

The authors are pleased to acknowledge many fruitful interactions with numerous colleagues, in particular Jean Arlat, Alain Costes, Yves Deswarte, Cliff Jones, and especially with fellow members of IFIP WG 10.4 on Dependable Computing and Fault Tolerance. Early part of this work received support from the CNRS-NSF grant "Tolerance to intentional faults."

References

[1]   T.F. Arnold, "The Concept of Coverage and Its Effect on the Reliability Model of Repairable Systems," IEEE Trans. Computers, **vol. 22**, no. 6, pp. 251-254, June 1973.

[2]   D. Avresky, J. Arlat, J.C. Laprie, and Y. Crouzet, "Fault Injection for Formal Testing of Fault Tolerance," IEEE Trans. Reliability, **vol. 45**, no. 3, pp. 443-455, Sept. 1996.

[3]   A. Avizienis, "Design of Fault-Tolerant Computers," Proc. 1967 Fall Joint Computer Conf., AFIPS Conf. Proc., **vol. 31**, pp. 733-743, 1967.

[4]   A. Avizienis and L. Chen, "On the Implementation of N-Version Programming for Software Fault Tolerance During Execution," Proc. IEEE COMPSAC 77 Conf., pp. 149-155, Nov. 1977.

[5]   A. Avizienis and Y. He, "Microprocessor Entomology: A Taxonomy of Design Faults in COTS Microprocessors," Dependable Computing for Critical Applications 7, C.B. Weinstock and J. Rushby, eds., pp. 3-23, 1999.

[6]   A. Avizienis and J.P.J. Kelly, "Fault Tolerance by Design Diversity: Concepts and Experiments," Computer, **vol. 17**, no. 8, pp. 67-80, Aug. 1984.

[7]   B.W. Boehm, "Guidelines for Verifying and Validating Software Requirements and Design Specifications," Proc. European Conf. Applied Information Technology (IFIP '79), pp. 711-719, Sept. 1979.

[8]   W.G. Bouricius, W.C. Carter, and P.R. Schneider, "Reliability Modeling Techniques for Self-Repairing Computer Systems," Proc. 24th Nat'l Conf. ACM, pp. 295-309, 1969.

[9]   C. Cachin, J. Camenisch, M. Dacier, Y. Deswarte, J. Dobson, D. Horne, K. Kursawe, J.C. Laprie, J.C. Lebraud, D. Long, T. McCutcheon, J. Muller, F. Petzold, B. Pfitzmann, D. Powell, B. Randell, M. Schunter, V. Shoup, P. Verissimo, G. Trouessin, R.J. Stroud, M. Waidner, and I. Welch, "Malicious- and Accidental-Fault Tolerance in Internet Applications: Reference Model and Use Cases," LAAS report no. 00280, MAFTIA, Project IST-1999-11583, p. 113, Aug. 2000.

[10] V. Castelli, R.E. Harper, P. Heidelberger, S.W. Hunter, K.S. Trivedi, K. Vaidyanathan, and W.P. Zeggert, "Proactive Management of Software Aging," IBM J. Research and Development, **vol. 45**, no. 2, pp. 311-332, Mar. 2001.

[11] "Termes et Définitions Concernant la Qualité de Service, la Disponibilité et la fiabilité,"Recommandation G 106, CCITT, 1984.

[12] Information Technology Security Evaluation Criteria, Harmonized criteria of France, Germany, the Netherlands, the United Kingdom, Commission of the European Communities, 1991.

[13] R. Chillarege, I.S. Bhandari, J.K. Chaar, J. Halliday, D.S. Moebus, B.K. Ray, and M.-Y. Wong, "Orthogonal Defect Classification-A Concept for In-Process Measurements," IEEE Trans. Software Eng., **vol. 18**, no. 11, pp. 943-956, Nov. 1992.

[14] F. Cristian, "Understanding Fault-Tolerant Distributed Systems," Comm. ACM, **vol. 34**, no. 2, pp. 56-78, 1991.

[15] H. Debar, M. Dacier, M. Nassehi, and A. Wespi, "Fixed vs. Variable- Length Patterns for Detecting Suspicious Process Behavior," Proc. Fifth European Symp. Research in Computer Security, Sept. 1998.

[16] R.J. Ellison, D.A. Fischer, R.C. Linger, H.F. Lipson, T. Longstaff, and N.R. Mead, "Survivable Network Systems: An Emerging Discipline," Technical Report CMU/SEI-97-TR-013, Carnegie Mellon Univ., May 1999.

[17] J.C. Fabre, V. Nicomette, T. Perennou, R.J. Stroud, and Z. Wu, "Implementing Fault Tolerant Applications Using Reflective Object-Oriented Programming," Proc 25th IEEE Int'l Symp. Fault-Tolerant Computing (FTCS-25), pp. 489-498, 1995.

[18] S. Forrest, S.A. Hofmeyr, A. Somayaji, and T.A. Longstaff, "A Sense of Self for Unix Processes," Proc. 1996 IEEE Symp. Security and Privacy, pp. 120-128, May 1996.

[19] A. Fox and D. Patterson, "Self-Repairing Computers," Scientific Am., vol. 288, no. 6, pp. 54-61, 2003.

[20] J.M. Fray, Y. Deswarte, and D. Powell, "Intrusion Tolerance Using Fine-Grain Fragmentation-Scattering," Proc. 1986 IEEE Symp. Security and Privacy, pp. 194-201, Apr. 1986.

[21] "Fundamental Concepts of Fault Tolerance," Proc. 12th IEEE Int'l Symp. Fault-Tolerant Computing (FTCS-12), pp. 3-38, June 1982.

[22] A.G. Ganek and T.A. Korbi, "The Dawning of the Autonomic Computing Era," IBM Systems J., **vol. 42**, no. 1, pp. 5-18, 2003.

[23] J.N. Gray, "Why do Computers Stop and What Can Be Done About It?" Proc. Fifth Symp. Reliability in Distributed Software and Database Systems, pp. 3-12, Jan. 1986.

[24] J. Gray, "Functionality, Availability, Agility, Manageability, Scalability—the New Priorities of Application Design," Proc. Int'l Workshop High Performance Trans. Systems, Apr. 2001.

[25] R. Grigonis, "Fault-Resilience for Communications Convergence," Special Supplement to CMP Media's Converging Comm. Group, Spring 2001.

[26] J.E. Hosford, "Measures of Dependability," Operations Research, **vol. 8**, no. 1, pp. 204-206, 1960.

[27] Y. Huang, C. Kintala, N. Kolettis, and N.D. Fulton, "Software Rejuvenation: Analysis, Module and Applications," Proc. 25th IEEE Int'l Symp. Fault-Tolerant Computing, pp. 381-390, June 1995.

[28] Y. Huang and C. Kintala, "Software Fault Tolerance in the Application Layer," Software Fault Tolerance, M. Lyu, ed., pp. 231-248, 1995.

[29] Industrial-Process Measurement and Control—Evaluation of System Properties for the Purpose of System Assessment, Part 5: Assessment of System Dependability, Draft, Publication 1069-5, Int'l Electrotechnical Commission (IEC) Secretariat, Feb. 1992.

[30] "Functional Safety of Electical/Electronic/Programmable Electronic Safety-Related Systems," IEC Standard 61505, 1998.

[31] "Quality Concepts and Terminology," part 1: Generic Terms and Definitions, Document ISO/TC 176/SC 1 N 93, Feb. 1992.

[32] "Common Criteria for Information Technology Security Evaluation," ISO/IEC Standard 15408, Aug. 1999.

[33] J. Jacob, "The Basic Integrity Theorem," Proc. Int'l Symp. Security and Privacy, pp. 89-97, 1991.

[34] J. Johnson, "Chaos: The Dollar Drain of IT Project Failures," Application Development Trends, pp. 41-47, Jan. 1995.

[35] M.K. Joseph and A. Avizienis, "A Fault Tolerance Approach to Computer Viruses," Proc. Symp. Security and Privacy, pp. 52-58, Apr. 1988.

[36] M.K. Joseph and A. Avizienis, "Software Fault Tolerance and Computer Security: A Shared Problem," Proc. Ann. Joint Conf. Software Quality and Reliability, pp. 428-432, Mar. 1988.

[37] "DBench Dependability Benchmarks," DBench, Project IST-2000-25425, K. Kanoun et al., eds., pp. 233, May 2004.

[38] L. Lamport, R. Shostak, and M. Pease, "The Byzantine Generals Problem," ACM Trans. Programming Languages and Systems, **vol. 4**, no. 3, pp. 382-401, July 1982.

[39] C.E. Landwher, A.R. Bull, J.P. McDermott, and W.S. Choi, "A Taxonomy of Computer Program Security Flaws," ACM Computing Survey, **vol. 26**, no. 3, pp. 211-254, 1994.

[40] J.C. Laprie, "Dependable Computing and Fault Tolerance: Concepts and Terminology," Proc. 15th IEEE Int'l Symp. Fault-Tolerant Computing (FTCS-15), pp. 2-11, June 1985.

[41] Dependability: Basic Concepts and Terminology, J.C. Laprie, ed., Springer-Verlag, 1992.

[42] J.C. Laprie, "Dependability—Its Attributes, Impairments and Means," Predictably Dependable Computing Systems, B. Randell et al., eds., pp. 3-24, 1995.

[43] N.A. Lynch, Distributed Algorithms. Morgan Kaufmann, 1996.

[44] J. McLean, "A Comment on the 'Basic Security Theorem' of Bell and LaPadula," Information Processing Letters, **vol. 20**, no. 2, pp. 67-70, 1985.

[45] J.F. Meyer, "On Evaluating the Performability of Degradable Computing Systems," Proc. Eighth IEEE Int'l Symp. Fault-Tolerant Computing (FTCS-8), pp. 44-49, June 1978.

[46] J. Musa, "The Operational Profile in Software Reliability Engineering: An Overview," Proc. Third IEEE Int'l Symp. Software Reliability Eng. (ISSRE '92), pp. 140-154, 1992.

[47] An Introduction to Computer Security: The NIST Handbook, Special Publication 800-12, Nat'l Inst. of Standards and Technology, 1995.

[48] National Science and Technology Council, "Information Technology Frontiers for a New Millennium,"Supplement to the Prsident's FY 2000 Budget, 2000.

[49] R. Ortalo, Y. Deswarte, and M. Kaaniche, "Experimenting with Quantitative Evaluation Tools for Monitoring Operational Security," IEEE Trans. Software Eng., **vol. 25**, no. 5, pp. 633-650, Sept./Oct. 1999.

[50] D. Parnas, "On the Criteria to be Used in Decomposing Systems into Modules," Comm. ACM, **vol. 15**, no. 12, pp. 1053-1058, Dec. 1972.

[51] M.C. Paulk, B. Curtis, M.B. Chrissis, and C.V. Weber, "Capability Maturity Model for Software," Technical Reports CMU/SEI-93-TR-24, ESC-TR-93-177, Software Eng. Inst., Carnegie Mellon Univ., Feb. 1993.

[52] C.P. Pfleeger, "Data Security," Encyclopedia of Computer Science, A. Ralston et al., eds., Nature Publishing Group, pp. 504-507, 2000.

[53] D. Powell, G. Bonn, D. Seaton, P. Verissimo, and F. Waeselynck, "The Delta-4 Approach to Dependability in Open Distributed Computing Systems," Proc. 18th IEEE Int'l Symp. Fault-Tolerant Computing (FTCS-18), pp. 246-251, June 1988.

[54] D. Powell, "Failure Mode Assumptions and Assumption Coverage," Proc. 22nd IEEE Int'l Symp. Fault-Tolerant Computing (FTCS-22), pp. 386-395, June 1992.

[55] "Conceptual Model and Architecture of MAFTIA,"MAFTIA, Project IST-1999-11583, D. Powell and R. Stroud, eds., p. 123, Jan. 2003.

[56] M.O. Rabin, "Efficient Dispersal of Information for Security, Load Balancing and Fault Tolerance," J. ACM, **vol. 36**, no. 2, pp. 335-348, Apr. 1989.

[57] B. Randell, "System Structure for Software Fault Tolerance," IEEE Trans. Software Eng., **vol. 1**, no. 2, pp. 220-232, June 1975.

[58] "Software Considerations in Airborne Systems and Equipment Certification,"DO-178-B/ED-12-B, Requirements and Technical Concepts for Aviation/European Organization for Civil Aviation Equipement, 1992.

[59] J. Rushby, "Formal Specification and Verification of a Fault-Masking and Transient-Recovery Model for Digital Flight Control Systems," Proc. Second Int'l Symp. Formal Techniques in Real Time and Fault-Tolerant Systems, 1992.

[60] J. Rushby, "Formal Methods and Their Role in the Certification of Critical Systems," Technical Report CSL-95-1, SRI Int'l, 1995.

[61] W.H. Sanders, M. Cukier, F. Webber, P. Pal, and R. Watro, "Probabilistic Validation of Intrusion Tolerance," Supplemental Volume Int'l Conf. Dependable Systems and Networks (DSN-2002), pp. 78-79, June 2002.

[62] Trust in Cyberspace. F. Schneider, ed., Nat'l Academy Press, 1999.

[63] D.P. Siewiorek and R.S. Swarz, Reliable Computer Systems, Design and Evaluation. Digital Press, 1992.

[64] R.M. Smith, K.S. Trivedi, and A.V. Ramesh, "Performability Analysis: Measures, an Algorithm, and a Case Study," IEEE Trans. Computers, **vol. 37**, no. 4, pp. 406-417, Apr. 1988.

[65] "Dependability Assessment Criteria," SQUALE project (ACTS95/AC097), LAAS Report no. 98456, Jan. 1999.

[66] P. Thevenod-Fosse, H. Waeselynck, and Y. Crouzet, "An Experimental Study on Softawre Structural Testing: Deterministic Testing Versus Random Input Generation," Proc. 21st IEEE Int'l Symp. Fault-Tolerant Computing, pp. 410-417, June 1981.

[67] USA Department of Transportation, Office of Inspector General, "Audit Report: Advance Automation System,"Report AV-1998-113, Apr. 1998.

[68] A. Valdes, M. Almgren, S. Cheung, Y. Deswarte, B. Dutertre, J. Levy, H. Saïdi, V. Stavridou, and T. Uribe, "An Adaptative Intrusion-Tolerant Server Architecture," Proc. 10th Int'l Workshop Security Protocols, Apr. 2002.

[69] E.J. Weyuker, "On Testing Nontestable Programs," The Computer J., **vol. 25**, no. 4, pp. 465-470, 1982.

[70] A. Wood, "NonStop Availability in a Client/Server Environment," Tandem Technical Report 94.1, Mar. 1994.

A Process for Developing a Common Vocabulary in the Information Security Area
J. von Knop et al. (Eds.)
IOS Press, 2007

Blueprint of a Security Glossary:
A Common Language for Creating
International Security Policies

Sanjay GOEL

University at Albany, SUNY 1400 Washington Avenue, Albany, NY 12222
Email: goel@albany.edu

Abstract. Close coordination among law enforcement agencies, researchers, and intelligence agencies is required to solve the problem of computer crime. There are several barriers to this cooperation including asymmetric laws, national interests, and poor communication mechanisms. Computers have not only led to new types of crimes, but have provided additional avenues for existing crimes. Laws for traditional crimes have not evolved quickly enough to accommodate technology developments. To foster increased cooperation, it is necessary to have a common vocabulary, which will avoid confusion in interpretation of laws, security policies, data, and research due to differences in language, vocabulary, and semantics. The basic premise of the paper is that security policies are the key instrument of security that will help in tacking international cybercrime and a shared vision of security would be achieved through common security policies. This paper presents recommendations and results from the creation of an initial security glossary compiled from public sources on the Internet as a part of research in developing metrics for information security policies. The large variation in terminology and definitions underscores the necessity of standardization of nomenclature in security.

1. Introduction

Information security has become an international problem requiring active cooperation among researchers and law enforcement officials to collect data, provide security tools, and solve computer-related crimes. The Internet spans across geographical boundaries and criminals can launch sophisticated attacks without physical proximity to the location of a crime. Internet attacks are not only a forte of bored hackers looking for excitement, but also a useful device for organized crime syndicates and militant terrorist groups. Such attacks are also becoming a tool of state-sponsored espionage and for white-collar financial crimes such as fraud and embezzlement.

The fundamental problem with securing the Internet is due to its biggest virtue— its openness. No one has complete authority or control over the Internet, and users and machines are constantly added and removed. The Internet is like a community with multiple neighborhoods (or networks) where each house represents a computer. New houses can be added to the neighborhoods and people move in and out of the houses. While a neighborhood needs to be protected, so too do the individual houses that make up the neighborhood, and the people who live in the houses. Security thus has to be multi-leveled and distributed. The technology on which the Internet is built was intended for open communication and not to conduct business, and consequently, security is an afterthought rather than an integral part of the infrastructure. Given such an infrastructure, security can be managed but not guaranteed.

Security is typically managed by the implementation of security policies introduced at both the system and organizational levels. System security policies govern the entities in software, computer, and networks while organizational security policies govern the deployment and management of computing infrastructure as well as user behavior in an organization. Sufficient formalism exists at the system level, which provides universal consistency in the application of security policies. Security policies at the system level govern rational entities with predictable behavior allowing for verification of security. At the organizational level, however, application of security policies is chaotic. An organizational security policy governs passionate entities (humans) that are inherently untrustworthy due to their unpredictability. The implementation of such policies requires an understanding not only of the policy, but also the context in which policy is applied, and needs to be enforced with deterrents as well as incentives. It is evident that in such an environment where the context can vary significantly across the organization including expertise of users, mission of the organization and relevant legislation communication becomes critical. It is thus understandable that while security policies are universally applied, they differ considerably across organizations. However, this lack of consistency is also found in both the syntax as well as semantics of the policies. The syntax of the policy refers to its content structure and organization while the semantics deals with the interpretation of the elements of the policy. For instance, a security policy may suggest that the computer "may be quarantined". The word "quarantine" may be interpreted as take if off the network or to leave it untouched and shutdown so that the log files do not change. Similarly, people may refer to a computer program as code, software, program, or executable. The word "code" may mean a completely different thing to a cryptographer compared to an information security expert.

De facto standards for security policies are emerging in different countries across the globe and have many associated problems. These are: 1) existence of multiple standards, 2) vagueness in their interpretation, 3) lack of consistency of terminology, 4) rapid obsolescence of standards due to fast changing technology, and 5) lack of metrics for measuring the impact of standards and policies. Applying security policies indiscriminately without understanding their impact in context of the organization is neither economical nor effective. Implementing security across geographic borders requires coordination among users, law enforcement agencies, researchers, and system administrators. It is important for these groups to understand and speak the same language. Professionals in the security field understand the terminology due to their training and experience. However, a majority of users find the terminology vague and ambiguous. Even law enforcement officers are daunted by the task of learning security jargon and keeping abreast of technological change. A better conceptual understanding of the technology will allow the entire community to share the burden of maintaining security on the Internet and securing its borders.

The Internet contains hundreds of security glossaries that define security terms with various definitions. There are considerable differences based on context of the glossary, e.g., linguistics, technical, legal, law enforcement etc. There are also differences within the same context in both the level of detail as well as the definitions themselves. The first step towards standardization of terminology would be collaboratively building a glossary that contains the vocabulary and definitions for important security-related terms and concepts. This glossary should also list popular synonyms to ensure no ambiguity between similar terms and acronyms since they are an integral part of communication. The complexity surrounding information security stems from its multidisciplinary affiliations, including computer science, business, law, psychology, etc. Terms arise in different fields and then are interpreted by researchers in disparate areas. Building consensus across different disciplines is certainly desirable but is not feasible in the near future, but within each discipline consensus can typically built through a sustained debate among experts.

The problem of interpretation becomes worse when translation to multiple languages occurs. Literal translation of words from different languages can lead to ambiguity due to variations in context and culture. Consequently, it is important to create mappings between glossaries in different languages. Researchers and linguists from different countries can help in bridging this gap of understanding between glossaries of different languages. In addition, there needs to be standardization in the security policy syntax and semantics. To facilitate sharing of intelligence, standardization of data collection procedures and storage is necessary. Such intelligence data will also support research in creating more accurate detection tools and providing early warning for impending attacks.

This paper discusses the evolution of cybercrime and presents mechanisms to address the growing menace of crime, i.e., common information security glossary. The paper is organized as follows: Section 2 describes how crime is evolving in the Internet era; Section 3 presents a blueprint for a multilingual common security glossary and Section 4 presents some concluding remarks.

2. The Changing Nature of Crime

The Internet has not only led to creation of new types of crimes, but is also serving as an alternate channel for criminals to commit traditional crimes. Computer-related crimes can be broadly differentiated into three categories: 1) crimes against computer systems, 2) crimes against communications systems, and 3) crimes facilitated by computers and the Internet ([2]). Crimes against computer systems (computer crime) typically refer to unauthorized access of proprietary data or use of services on a computer without authorized consent of the user. It may also involve dissemination or storage of illegal information such as child pornography or relaying of offensive messages through computer networks. In the United States, the principal federal criminal law protecting computer systems is the Computer Fraud and Abuse Act (CFAA). Crimes against communications systems involve transmission of data, including, voice, images, and text through any media, including, radio, electromagnetic, and photo-optical. United States has several existing laws on interception of communication for both wired and wireless media. In most relevant act is the Electronic Communications Privacy Act of 1986 (ECPA) that was enacted to make existing laws more relevant to communications through computers and networks. Crimes facilitated by computers and networks involve the use of a computer to facilitate the crime, i.e., gathering information for crime or using a computer to transmit information. Sometimes it is difficult to distinguish between computer crime and computer-assisted crime and in many cases, both a computer crime and a computer-assisted crime occur together. For instance, a hacker may break into someone else's computer (computer crime) and use the computer to harass someone through threatening emails (computer-assisted crime). There is a wide spectrum of computer crimes, including, theft of data, disruption of services, illegal use of resources, and intellectual property theft. They can be generally classified into three major categories, i.e., fraud, pornography and obscenity, and infringement of intellectual property rights. Laws have existed for fraud and pornography for a long time. These laws are being interpreted and tested for crime cases involving computers. In addition, Congress passed the Digital Millennium Copyright Act (DMCA) in 1988 to address the issue of copyright infringement in response to piracy of music and software. New vectors of computer crimes are also emerging rapidly. One of the fastest growing segments of cybercrime is social crime including cyber stalking, dissemination of child pornography, and harassment. In addition, one crime can facilitate perpetrating of another crime, e.g., theft of data can be done via hacking, spyware, and misuse of privileges, and illegal use of resources can occur via botnets, breaching network security, and password theft.

Solving computer crime is a difficult problem that is rooted in a deep understanding of computers and networks as well as in law. The technology is still evolving and the laws are still emerging. Organizations need to stay abreast of the laws and be able to manage their technology in compliance with the law in disparate areas, such as, privacy, copyright, money laundering criminal negligence. Security policies have become an instrument that unravel through the technical and legal morass into clear plain language that can be implemented and enforced. Security policies form a bridge between user compliance and security legislation. Ensuring consistency, clarity, as well as accuracy of security policies is thus critical to foster user compliance with security legislation. In addition, since computer crime has international bearings ensuring their consistent interpretation across linguistic and geographic barriers is vital to ensuring security.

Although there have been efforts to create standardized international policies, i.e. the Agreement on Trade-Related Aspects of Intellectual Property Rights (TRIPS), these have been difficult to put into practice. The problem is not global will, but rather global implementation and the same is true for universal policies created for computer-related crimes. International cooperation among law enforcement agencies is essential to making serious breakthroughs in tackling these Internet-based crimes, which are perpetrated across vast geographic areas with various jurisdictions. One threat that has increased the need for cooperation among multi-national law enforcement and intelligence agencies is terrorism. Terrorists are using the Internet for coordination, logistics, propaganda, and money laundering. Terrorist websites continually shift their identity by changing their location, names, and content to avoid detection. For cases of terrorism involving logistics and coordination, a prompt response is important to prevent heinous attacks from being committed. Tracking other terrorist activities such as money laundering requires a methodical tracing of transactions through electronic fund transfers to determine patterns of behavior that suggest illegal activities. Several bilateral treaties have been created among countries for sharing intelligence and cooperating in tracking terrorist activities through the Internet. However, bilateral treaties are insufficient since universal laws that cover the entire globe are required as elucidated below through a scenario involving terrorist activity.

Let us consider the case of terrorism where meticulous international planning occurs with commanders sitting in remote parts of the world launching sophisticated attacks on major cities. Such attacks are a result of painstaking planning, coordination, and communication. The trail forms a complex web that spans several countries including activities such as money laundering, weapons smuggling, illegal immigration, and forgery of documents. Clues of terrorist activity are hidden in data logs spread across the globe. Without a seamless set of laws, uninhibited cooperation, and standardization of our practices, it is virtually impossible to sort through the intricate details of their activities to predict their activities and difficult trace those after the attacks are committed.

A major step towards international cooperation was the Council of Europe Convention on Cybercrime. The convention emphasized the need for cooperation among law enforcement as well as to create uniform international laws for computer-related crimes. The convention resulted in the "Convention on Cybercrime" treaty in 2001, which was ratified recently by the United States Senate in August 2006 (Convention, 2001). The purpose of this treaty was for collaborating in computer crime and requires ratifying members to enact legislation in several areas, including, illegal access, illegal interception of computer data, data interference, system interference, misuse of devices, computer-related fraud and forgery, child pornography, and copyright violations (on a commercial scale). The need for cooperation to solve international crimes is well accepted the challenge now is to put the treaty into practice. There are several impediments to implementing the provisions of the treaty, such as, discrepancy in crime legislation, lack of technological capability, and a need to balance social and cultural norms with law enforcement needs, and political will.

Creation of shared international laws is construed as a precursor to international cooperation. However, political, social, and cultural compulsions will make the creation of common laws a long and onerous process. Let us take the case of child pornography. Different countries have different legal age of sexual consent. While an image could be construed as legitimate in one country, does it become illegal as it cross borders? In this instance, does the distributor of the image become a criminal upon crossing geographic borders? Creating universal laws across the globe though very desirable is not feasible in the near future. Laws are based on the social context of the countries where they are enacted to reflect their constitutional rights and social norms. Political, social, and cultural compulsions will make the creation of common laws a long and onerous process. In addition, the process of enacting laws can be quite different across nations and harmonization of laws may be a task that lawmakers find difficult. In the United States alone, there numerous pieces of new legislation related to computer crimes in (Brenner, 2001). It is difficult to build consensus within a nation let alone across multiple nations. However, as the world changes and technology brings people closer together, we have no choice but to accept the challenge of attempting to create harmonious laws that can be universally applied. In order to implement international security policies effectively, there needs to be sufficient time to overcome political, social, and cultural barriers. While the process of creating international laws continues, several things can be done to remove barriers to communication and ease the implementation of laws once they are enacted. These include a shared vocabulary, standard data collection mechanisms, and a standard language for creating security policies as discussed in the following sections.

3. Security Informatics and Sharing Intelligence

As crime takes on a more international connotation, sharing security data among law enforcement and intelligence agencies across geographical borders becomes essential. Sharing of data poses a challenge to agencies even in the same country, for reasons such as privacy laws, lack of trust among agencies, lack of resources, and incompatibility of information systems. It becomes even more difficult to share data among countries because of conflicts of interest, political compulsions, and technological barriers. The other problem in sharing data is sheer volume. Data is growing at a very rapid rate, and sorting and sifting through all the garbage data to find a few nuggets of useful information becomes a daunting task.

There is an intricate network of crimes including child trafficking, terrorism, drug trade, money laundering, and logistics. Criminals are camouflaging their activities very carefully under a veil of legitimate businesses that may seem innocuous at first glance. By correlating information from multiple sources, patterns emerge that help in the detection of criminal activities. Let us take the example of money laundering which is really at the core of a lot of crime. Money laundering is used either to transfer funds from illegal activities such as drug running and smuggling or to support illegal activities such as espionage and terrorism. Most countries have clear laws prohibiting money laundering; however, this practice continues with 2-5% of the international GDP consisting of laundered money. Money laundering involves complex transactions that pass through organizations such as, real estate agencies, insurance companies, charitable organizations, and brokers worldwide. While the transactions at each institution may appear legitimate, a connection or a set of transactions together can reveal a money laundering operation. Since the operations are international, it requires sharing of information between businesses and government, national governments, and financial institutions across the globe. Differences in their legislation, compliance requirements, bank secrecy laws, and judicial interpretations need to be overcome in order to share data effectively. Techniques are required for efficient collection, aggregation, and classification of data. Without having standard templates and formats for collection, the process of integration of data becomes arduous and infeasible except for the worst crimes such as drug trafficking or terrorism. The next few sections discuss explicit tasks that can address some of the communication issues discussed above, i.e., common security glossary, standard language for security policy creation, shared templates, and a repository of security data for law enforcement and research.

3.1 Multilingual Security Glossary

Our ability to prevent cybercrime and track down its perpetrators is seriously hampered by a lack of communication among security agencies. Solving criminal cases is often a cumbersome process that requires collection of evidence from electronic media and maintaining accurate timeline of events. This requires an understanding of the technology as well as experience in evidence gathering and preserving. As a first step to improved communication and proper training for the personnel involved in fighting computer crime a glossary is required that defines the proper nomenclature as well as definitions. Compiling a glossary is a painstaking process that involves identifying all the terms in a domain and then building a consensus on the meanings of the terms. A glossary is a standardized list of commonly used terms in a specific domain and their universal definitions. Such a glossary would also assist in ensuring that the system administrators understand the security requirements clearly and that the users understand the security restrictions. A majority of computer breaches is due to human error due to indifference, carelessness, and laziness, however, a lack of understanding of the technology contributes to this. Clarification of the terminology is the first step towards creating better understand and synergy among the different stakeholders.

As the field of information security has evolved, the terminology associated with it has changed as well. As new terms and concepts are introduced into the vocabulary, communication becomes difficult. This is especially true when translations occur across multiple languages and result in confusion of the intended definitions and concepts. The first step in eliminating this ambiguity is to create a common security glossary that is universally acceptable. In the past, glossaries have been created by groups of experts who work together to identify the terms in the domain and build consensus in the terminology. Though very effective, such an endeavor is becoming harder due to the fast evolution in the field as well as the breadth of the field. Internet is rapidly becoming a source of information for people looking to get terminology and definitions.

The problem we face is not a lack of glossaries, but rather a proliferation of them. A search of the term "security glossary" using the Google search engine retrieves over 39 million English results alone. This proliferation of glossaries reflects a lack of standardization and consistency in terminology. To understand this proliferation, we conducted a study to evaluate the security glossaries available on the Internet ([Goel & Chengalur-Smith, 2006]). The compiled glossary was used to create metrics for security policies wherein the level of technical content in a policy was computed by counting the number of technical terms from the glossary that were included in the policy.

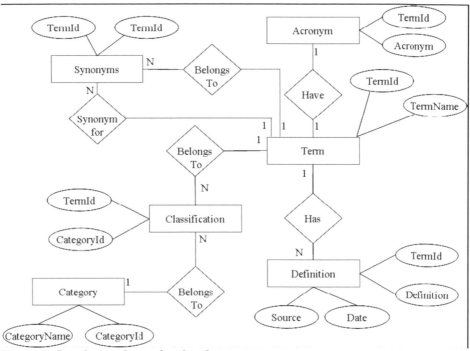

Figure 1. Database schema for the glossary.

To compile the master glossary, twelve glossaries were selected from reliable sources including dominant Internet companies such as Microsoft, government agencies such as National Institute of Standards and Testing, and security research organizations such as SANS. The glossaries were selected using the Google search engine on the Internet. The glossaries varied in size from 22 to 496 with the mean number of terms 167 and a standard deviation of 132. A relational database of security terms in the glossaries was created and a schema for the database is presented in Figure 1. The database links the terms from different glossaries to their definitions and source. In addition, it contains a list of acronyms that are defined in the glossaries. The term table is the most important table that links to the acronyms, definitions, and the categories. A self-referencing many-to-many relationship between a term and its synonym is defined as each term can have other synonyms in the database. Although not all terms have acronyms, when they exist they are uniquely matched to a given term, hence the one-to one relationship among those tables. Each term on an average has 1.33 definitions with the maximum number of definitions being 9 and minimum being 1. Though sufficient for the purpose of creating metrics, the master glossary demonstrates the variability in the terminology quite elegantly underscoring the necessity of consensus building. One way of building consensus is the use of the Wiki technology where the public or a group of experts can come together in an electronic forum to create such a vocabulary. Opening such an effort to public is fraught with danger of creating an unmanageable situation of too many opinions where it will become virtually impossible to reach a consensus. A controlled group of experts would perhaps server better to create a shared vocabulary.

The database contains 1515 terms, 26 synonyms, 140 acronyms, and 2006 definitions. Several of the glossaries did not provide definitions while others provided definitions for some of the terms. The acronyms and synonyms are critical since they add to the confusion of the users when terms are used interchangeably in the literature or the same acronym exists in some other field. The problem also arises because the terms are quite often lumped together without being classified into sub-categories. Classification of terms helps in creating a compact representation of the terminology and a better conceptual understanding of the domain. The categories were determined by analyzing the distinct security policies that are typically enacted in organizations. As shown in Table 1, 20 classification levels were created. Several of the terms were in multiple categories due to their relevance.

Network Security	Application Security	Communication Media (Phone, Fax)	Risk Analysis
Internet	Software Development	Storage Media, and Documentation	Legal Compliance
E-mail / IM	Access Control	Acceptable Use	Incident Handling
Online Transactions (B2B, B2C & Internal Transactions)	Monitoring (Audits, Synchronization, Log Analysis, etc.)	Information Exchange (file transfer, p2p)	Environmental Control
Malicious code	Authentication	Encryption	Physical Security

Table 1: List of Categories for Security Terms

The database exhibits some natural inter-relationships within the terms, which suggests that the glossary should be extended into ontology. The ontology is typically defined as a controlled vocabulary that describes objects and the relations between them in a formal way, and has a grammar for using the vocabulary terms. Ontologism figure prominently in the semantic web as a way of representing the semantics of documents and enabling the semantics to be used by web applications. Ontologism are also useful for a community as a way of structuring and defining the meaning of the metadata terms that are currently being collected and standardized. The security glossary could encompass key concepts and terminology that can be hierarchically organized into a meaningful taxonomy. A multilingual ontology in security would help propagate a shared vocabulary across different communities including, researchers, users, and law enforcement officials. As the field changes, the ontology should evolve keeping pace with the technology. Perhaps a good way of ensuring that the ontology is current is to create a schedule for updating and revising the ontology. A standard ontology would prevent redundancy through proliferation of semi-accurate term definitions on the Internet and held create a shared common understanding of information security. This paper elucidates the concept and shows the necessity of such an effort, the development of a workable ontology would require global cooperation among researchers and language experts across multiple countries.

4. Discussion and Future Work

It is important for organizations and law enforcement agencies to work cooperatively to control the rapidly rising incidence of computer-related crimes. Since they spans across geographical boundaries, a strong impetus exists for international cooperation in solving crimes. Policymakers often expound the necessity of enacting common international laws governing computer crime before making progress on solving international cybercrimes. The stark reality today is that differences in social, political, and cultural underpinnings of different nations make it difficult to create common international laws. Despite the lack of common laws, considerable progress could be made in computer-related crime detection and analysis by creating an infrastructure that facilitates communication and intelligence sharing both within countries and across countries. This paper proposes the creation of a standard nomenclature for sharing intelligence among law enforcement agencies. Specifically, it suggests creation of a common ontology that contains the terms, term definitions, and key concepts. The paper presents preliminary analysis of the problem of creating a common security glossary for security in the English language. Future work would include the expansion of terms and incorporation of terms and definitions in other languages.

References

[1]   An International Policy Framework for Internet Law Enforcement and Security: An Internet Alliance White Paper," May 2000, available at http://www.Internetalliance.org/policy/leswp.html
[2]   Appelman, Daniel, L., "Primer on Cybercrime Laws", ;login: August 2005.
[3]   Archick,.K., "Cybercrime: The Council of Europe Convention, "CRS Report for Congress Received through the CRS Web Updated December 1, 2005.
[4]   Brenner, Susan W., State Cybercrime Legislation in the United States of America: A Survey, 7 RICH. J.L. & TECH. 28 (Winter 2001), Available at http://www.richmond.edu/jolt/v7i3/article2.html.
[5]   CFAA, 18 USC § 1030 et seq., http://www.usdoj.gov/criminal/cybercrime/1030_new.html.
[6]   Convention on Cybercrime Treaty, Budapest, 23.XI.2001, Avalable at http://conventions.coe.int/ Treaty/en/Treaties/Html/185.htm

[7]   ECPA, 18 U.S.C. § 2510 et seq., http://www.usdoj.gov/criminal/cybercrime/wiretap2510_2522.htm.

[8]   Grove, Gregory D., Goodman, Seymour E., and Lukasik, Stephen J. "Cyber-attacks, Counter-attacks, and International Law," Survival 42 IISS, London, Autumn 2000.

[9]   International Coordination for Cybercrime and Terrorism in the 21st Century

[10] Sofaer, A.D, "Toward an International Convention on Cyber Security", Hoover Press: Cyber DP5 HPCYBE0600 06-09-:1 18:11:49 rev1 page 221

[11] United Nations Convention Against Illicit Traffic in Narcotic Drugs and Psychotropic Substances, December20, 1988, T.I.A.S.,20 I.L.M. 493 ("Narcotics Convention" or "Vienna Convention on Narcotics").

62

A Process for Developing a Common Vocabulary in the Information Security Area
J. von Knop et al. (Eds.)
IOS Press, 2007

Towards the creation of Security Ontologism for Information Technology, Communications, Information Systems, Information and Knowledge in Organizations

Dr. Paulo AMARAL

School of Economics and Management Catholic University of Portugal,
Palma de Cima 1649 023 Lisboa, Portugal

1. Introduction

This work discusses a methodological approach for developing a common international framework of understanding between researchers and practitioners of information security.

The increased rate of research and development in information systems alongside with the mass production and adoption of technology presents a major challenge regarding every security aspect. New hardware and new software, both for information processing and communication deserve new security approaches due to the security flaws that are inherent of every new system. Moreover, because systems are built more and more with system integration approaches, security flaws are inherited between systems with common roots. To make things worse, today's information systems are running more and more depending on each other networks, both within and between enterprises. Hence, asynchronous distributed systems are a reality that we have to embrace. For example, service oriented technologies a good example of this challenge. Consequently, the security measures have to evolve alongside with asynchronous distributed systems´ development.

The increased used of IS/IT for communication, mainly the widespread use of the Internet have created a major dependence of our societies on everything regarding technology, information and communication. IT is not by sheer chance that many authors claim that we are living in the Information Society [1]. The simple question of the millennium bug can give us an idea of our dependability on Information systems and Technology [2]. Security approaches must follow this increased dependability as well as the probability of attacks. Regarding the latter, the recent terrorist attacks in the United States, Spain and England and the recent dismantling of terrorist networks in Spain and in England also puts forward the importance of knowledge and information in the security area.

For the reasons put forward above, a new methodological approach is put forward in order to increase the capacity of understanding and then learning of the researchers and the practitioners of information security.

2. Discussion

The objective of this contribution is to draw action plans towards a better and flourishing common security framework. This aim could be easily and naïvely drawn by just proposing traditional working groups, projects, comities and steering comities to arrive to a common goal. The question here is that security has to evolve regarding its fundamental value and the value of each separate security item. Moreover, this evolution has to be adapted to the development of hardware, software, information systems and communications.

2.1 The importance of sharing a common view of information systems architecture

We can only secure what we know well. Even so, we may not be aware of some vulnerability. So let's start with security measures for what we supposedly know well.
A major aspect of this first issue is to create a common language, a common view and in the end a common understanding of what we are talking about. If a group of people is gong to cooperate in security issues, before security is discussed they should have in mind a common view of what is going to be protected.

Why and architecture? An architecture of concepts is the only way to be able to discuss a set on inter-related ideas. Information systems technology ahs been developed as an architectures. The first step in creating and understanding framework is to discuss and dominate the current information systems architectures and the most common instances of these, in the form of technological products. Most architectures have a common operating systems root due to the need of compatibility between architectural components. Therefore, Microsoft, IBM, Apple and UNIX based Open Systems architectures are among the first that have to be understood.

On top of this issue, security policies and strategies may then start to be discussed.

2.2 Security for the computing machine

Any computing machine is put up with hardware, on top of which runs an operating system that creates a virtual machine interface. In order to be used, this virtual machine needs a run-time environment. Security has to be addressed for each layer of the architecture [3].

The first technological issue to address within the architecture mentioned in the previous section is the virtual machine security with all of its components. A number of questions should be addressed here.

What are the current hardware architectures we are using and what are their security capabilities?

What are the current operating systems being used, what are their security capabilities and how do they use the security mechanisms provided by the respective hardware?

What are the characteristics of run-time systems and the most appropriate security policies?

In this context, for each of these virtual machines and each of these layers of the architecture, the discussion should address:
Physical security
Audit trail mechanisms
Risk assessment

Patch management
Authentication
Intrusion detection
Disaster recovery
Security tools
Incident handling
Encryption
 The base of any secure environment is set with the security provided by the virtual machine that handles the data and its computing.

2.3 Security for communications

Handling communication security is another major and important task. The communication infra-structure also has its architecture, and it should be in the context that the security has to be developed and discussed.

 We propose the use of the seven layered Open Standards Interconnection architecture [4].

 To communicate, the various nodes use instances of the seven layers in the form of communication protocols. Security discussion should address the communication protocols as a way to ensure the content.

 The communication protocols used nowadays all have their shortcomings and potential security breaches. Their development is phenomenal and we should include the new network capabilities like fibre optics and wireless networks or power line communication. For every communication device, for every communication protocol, we should consider their security policy.

 In this context, it is not hard to conceive a number of issues to discuss:
Viruses, Worms and Spyware
Encryption
Authentication
Intrusion detection
Security tools
Security policies
Auditing
Risk assessment
Web security
Laws and regulations
Certifications
Incident handling

2.4 Security for distributed systems

Security in the context of distributed systems is a most difficult issue to address [5]. First, the distributed system is conceived using the virtual machine and communication layers discussed above. Therefore, it starts to inherit the security characteristics of those, for better or for worse. But because a distributed system is, by definition, composed by a number of different actors, its security level is always limited by the weakest link.

 Moreover, distributed system security has to be managed using the technical elements of each one of its components, but it can not be managed incrementally [6].

The problem here with that a distributed system is, by definition loosely coupled and can not be defined statically for its components may even evolve in time.

Furthermore, the conception of information systems today is still much like art craft. It is not possible to ensure, in the vast majority of cases, that the system will behave completely as predicted. This is so simple because the way systems are developed nowadays is by trial an error. The development stops when most common errors are eliminated, but a number of minor errors and no conformities persist and span the distributed systems´ lifetime. The issue here and not only the minor errors (called most of the time, bugs) which are addressed by systems´ maintenance and version release policies, but the non conformities that keep hidden in the system. For example, the first Worm ever experienced in the Internet in 1988 was caused by a non conformity in the Ftp servers, called Ftp Deamons [7]. These are programs that run in the servers and allow clients to connect and download files from the Internet. These Ftp constitute a very simple quasi-synchronous distributed system. The question was that these software Deamons had a nonconformity that allowed intruders to spawn processes in background with administrator rights! The hacker of this Worm used this nonconformity to create processes that made client Ftp requests to all known servers of each machine in order to created other Worms in the form of spawned processes in the servers. The Code Red worm that caused a fuss a few years ago also used a similar mechanism with Microsoft code [8]. So, even if the communication and virtual machine layers are conveniently managed and secure, they cannot prevent completely the security breaches of the distributed systems.

There are two issues here. The first one is to discuss security policies of distributed system development and the second one, perhaps the most relevant, is to discuss the effective use of common distributed systems. The latter takes and enormous advantage from the collective experience of the community formed to collaborate in this issue.

2.5 Security for information and knowledge

"Information is what we extract from data regarding our previous knowledge"[Boisot 1995]. All issues discussed in the previous sections of this document deal with data security. Data will be transformed in information the moment it is used both for information acquisition, communication and also for decision making. Because the information consumption cycle is incremental, and transformation of data into information depends on the prior knowledge of the receiver, information security depends, not only on data, but also on the mechanisms that extract information from data and the learning mechanisms that create knowledge. These mechanisms exist beyond the boundaries of the computer and communications systems and include people.

Knowledge management is a fairly new discipline at the heart of organizations and societies. The knowledge concepts are much more difficult to tackle than simple technology because they involve social aspects which cannot be fully captured by scientific models whatsoever. Nevertheless, in order to act in ways that are more effective than just using plain common sense for decision making, there is a need for a scientific approach to help to understand this evolving and difficult reality involving mankind.

In the end, information and knowledge is what we should want to protect. Starting with data, both using computer and communications systems is only a first part, although important, of the security equation. The mechanisms that make people and organizations extract information from data and create knowledge through learning are absolutely fundamental for security. Moreover, information warfare, like cyberwar and netwar, as well as intelligence, are an important part of the security discussion.

Therefore, managing information security, more than just data, needs to be built upon a good understanding of what information and knowledge means in the context of the knowledge society.

Tackling information security should thus be built around an evolving architecture of concepts regarding information and knowledge. Our proposal is to discuss, at the same time, this architecture and the most appropriate security mechanisms for each layer.

2.6 The importance of a network for collaboration

One very important, even crucial, aspect of security management is collaboration. Today, this means using every communication mechanism to support the creation of common understanding.

There are two main reasons for the importance o network collaboration between all parties that what to help each other for security reasons:
To develop the learning abilities and the understanding of the IS/IT infrastructure, knowing that it is constantly changing and, perhaps even more important,
To learn about vulnerability and security measures on the fly, an quickly prepare defences and respond to security breaches.
There is no doubt that our learning abilities flourish in an environment of cooperation and collaboration.

An important contribution of our methodological contribution for developing security abilities is the creation of a broad community of expertise, which is able to learn together and develop new security doctrines together.

2.7 Security knowledge anthologies

Within the learning network put forward, the creation of common vocabularies is absolutely crucial for a common understanding.

The difficulty in creating vocabularies easily is the same of taxonomies and knowledge ontology [9]. Scientifically, there is a tendency to create taxonomies and to list the different concepts much like a dictionary with architecture to simplify the task.

We believe that security vocabularies need a methodological approach that can be best describes as the creation of knowledge ontology in a network environment. An example of the difficulty in grasping this task can be found in [10].

We find that there are three layers to manage for the creation of the knowledge ontology:
Knowledge repository
Groupware coordination - includes communication and decision making
Double loop – group level; strategy level
We present our views on the management of each of these layers and end by putting forward a methodology for the creation of security ontology.

2.7.1 Knowledge repository
The knowledge repository [11] has to be distributed which means coherent and accessible by all participants. It will have to be a database, with the explanation and the relationships between concepts. For a groupware approach creating this repository we

propose the use of WIKI technology. Furthermore, every item added in the repository would be followed by an editor which would accept and maintain each particular file version of the repository.

For building architecture of concepts, as already argued above, we propose the creation on the knowledge ontology using an appropriate metadata language like RDF. In this case an RDF editor would be required. We think that this may be the right direction to proceed because meaning is perhaps the most important feature necessary for the evolution of the knowledge society, for by having abundant data in the Internet, our thirst for knowledge keeps increasing. The *semantic web* [12] should be based on a metadata language, as an evolution of HTML and even XML, which already has metadata capabilities. The World Wide Web Consortium defined RDF [13] as the standard for the semantic Web.

2.7.2 Group Level Groupware Coordination

The different security concepts should be discussed by specialists in the different areas, in levels as described above. The discussion should follow the creation and evolution of the knowledge ontology as described. The theoretical concept behind the coordination of such groups should be a knowledge management approach known as communities of practice. This approach makes use of Intranets (using the Internet) and the use of groupware information systems to increase the communication and sharing among all participants.

One important methodological question is to consider distributed group dynamics because it will be an internationally distributed decision making context.

2.7.3 Strategic level Groupware Coordination

Because the security knowledge ontology is proposed to be created through layers of an architecture which corresponds to a number of groups cooperating internationally, there is a need to understand the comprehensiveness of the whole approach. A strategic coordination is needed for the cooperation and links between the various groups. Moreover, some the resources will be shared and also have to be coordinated.

The methodology for the groupware coordination of the various groups should rely on the mandatory participation of the head of each group and the voluntary participation of everyone involved.

2.7.4 Methodology for the development of security ontology

Our proposal is thus the creation of knowledge ontology for the security area using the following methodology:
Design phase
Define and formalise question
Define goals and objectives
Allocate resources
Define discussion methodology
Define coordination methodology
Development phase
Create ontology iteratively
Documentation and content management
Refine knowledge ontology tools in a distributed environment
Refine group dynamic coordination
Integration phase
Documentation revision preparation

Review models iteratively with experts
Expand models up on revision
Create semantic ontological representations
Validation phase

3. Conclusion

The creation of a vocabulary in the security area is absolutely necessary to enable free and effective communication among researchers and practitioners.

To develop security vocabularies in the information society, the evolving nature of the technological reality has to be taken into account. More than just a simple methodology that would create a dictionary of concepts we argue that the most important is the creation of network collaborative communities where individuals help each other to keep up to date, both technologically, and regarding security breaches and how to deal with them.

The creation of a security vocabulary is a socialized knowledge creation activity in a network multinational global environment. We propose a knowledge ontology approach for the creation of these security vocabularies.

The knowledge ontology methodology hereby proposed is in fact a way to grasp a view of a reality, which is always subjective, but whose model will increase significantly the ability to make informed decisions regarding security. Therefore, the methodology has to start from a good representation of a complex reality. We propose an architectural view to discuss in layers the various concepts that deal with the security of all elements that are part o the information life cycle, namely, data, information itself, and knowledge. For each one of these concepts, a number of issues should be discussed in view of the technological development in course. The architecture of computers, information systems and telecommunications, both fixed and wireless, is a starting point. Sociological questions that deal with information, knowledge management and intelligence should also be discussed as part of the security knowledge ontology.

References

[1]   S Crawford, The origin and development of a concept: the information society, Bull Med Libr Assoc. 1983
[2]   Ross Anderson, The Millennium Bug - Reasons not to Panic, University of Cambrige Computer Laboratory, 1999
[3]   The Protection of Information in Computer Systems, Jerome H. Saltzer, and Michael D. Schroeder, 1975
[4]   Huber Zimmerman, OS1 Reference Model-The IS0 Model of Architecture for Open Systems Interconnection, IEEE Transaction on Communications, Vol. 28, No. 4, April 1980
[5]   Butler W. Lampson, Martin Abadi, Michael Burrows, and Edward Wobber. Authentication in distributed systems: Theory and practice. ACM Transactions on Computer Systems, 10(4):265--310, November 1992
[6]   David White, Distributed Systems Security, DMBS 1997
[7]   Innovators of the Net: Ramanathan Gua and RDF, Marc Andreessen, Netscape Communications Corporation, 1999
[8]   D. Moore, C. Shannon, and J. Brown. Code-Red: a case study on the spread and victims of an Internet worm. In Proceedings of the 2002.
[9]   Gruber, T.R., Toward Principles for the Design of Ontologies Used for Knowledge Sharing, Int. Journal of Human-Computer Studies, Vol. 43, pp.907-928
[10]   Max Boisot, The Information Space, 1995

[11] Abecker, A., Bernardi, A., Hinkelmann, K., Kuhn, O. and Sintek, M. (1998), Towards a Technology for Organisational Memories, IEEE Intelligent Systems, 13(3) pp. 30-34.

[12] Semantic Web vision paper, Alexander Chislenko, June 1997

[13] Spafford, Eugene H. The Internet Worm Program: An Analysis . Technical Report CSD-TR-823. Department of Computer Science, Purdue University. November 1988.

[14] J. Vasconcelos, C Kimble & F. R. Gouveia, A design for a Group Memory System using Ontologies. Proceedings of 5th UKAIS Conference, University of Wales Institute, Cardiff, McGraw Hill, Forthcoming April 2000

A Process for Developing a Common Vocabulary in the Information Security Area
J. von Knop et al. (Eds.)
IOS Press, 2007

The Human Factor

Tim BREMMERS
Independent Justice and Home Affairs Consultant, the Netherlands

Ladies and gentlemen,

Thank you very much for entrusting me to share with you ideas and suggestions on what one[1] expects from the common glossary on information security. In the invitation for this event to me, it was said that from the answer it follows for example which terms should be included in the glossary.

I'll be frank with you: I have serious doubts here. Having been a police officer for some 30 years and having worked with many colleagues from many differing bodies originating from many differing countries and cultures, my experiences allow me to explain that:

If we talk information and information security, we talk commonly.

If we practice information and information security, we practice our own glossary.

So the key issue, to my opinion, is how to better co-operate, and in order to have the required results at the end of this process, we need to start at the beginning.

In my views information, and subsequently information security, are inextricably bound up with communication. For that reason, I invite you to join me on my travel through communication, information and information security, to wrap up my presentation with perhaps workable suggestions, contributing to the development of a Common Glossary in the Information Security Area.

Besides, talking communication it is good to realize that roughly 6,800 known languages and dialects are spoken in the (191?) countries of the world and that some 2,261 have writing systems (the others are only spoken) and about 300 of these have online dictionaries.
(Source: http://www.alphadictionary.com/langdir.html)

1. Personal introduction

As said, I've been a police officer for 30 years in the Netherlands. Since 1988 I've been engaged in international activities; first 5 years operationally with narcotics and intelligence and then 6 years particularly for the Dutch Police in the framework of cross border policing and the European Union's enlargement.

Since 1999 I'm full time committed to support local, cross border and regional functionalities of entities in the chain of justice, be it on the personal level or institutional level, be it within these entities or between entities, either in a uni-disciplinary or multi-disciplinary setting.

I'm absolutely independent and only accountable to myself, my wife, 4 children and – of course- my customers.

---

[1] "one" was first: "politicians"; not neglecting their relevance, role and responsibility, I believe they should not have the lead here, as too often politics blur

Through Dr. Alexey Salnikov, the NATO Russia Council Science Committee invited Tim Bremmers to participate at the Advanced Research Workshop. Me being a practitioner and certainly not a scientist I'm perhaps a stranger in your paradise.

However my views from the "outside" may contribute to the intended intense but informal exchange of views at the frontiers of the subject of the common vocabulary, aiming at identifying directions for future action in the area of information security.

2. Crises as energizers for solutions

We are all aware that crises boost both thinking and acting towards solutions of wearing problems, so I suggest identifying our crisis. My personal ones may now be known: I'm not a scientist; I've been a police-officer for 30 years, I'm Dutch by birth and I only speak 5 languages.

Our joint crisis is created by our limited perceptions:

	Things I see	Things I do not see
Things you see	Open for discussion	My blind spot
Things you do not see	Your blind spot	Shared blind spot

Fig. 1.

This one big problem is perhaps the most determining factor of the future development of the Common Vocabulary on Information Security, the latter to which I will refer as from now as C-VIS.

I already sarcastically referred to the experiences of common talking and individual acting; yet I believe this related to our main crisis:

We might feel insecure or unprofessional when we display or even worse, admit omissions and failures.

Not that I am without any form of shame but I allow you to follow my process of thinking to find solutions for these crises:

Crisis	Inversed	Reasonable Action	Next best RA
Not scientist	Scientist	Study science	Dialogue
30 years police	30 years no police	Reflect and assist	
Dutch	De-Dutch	Travel the world	Read
Only 5 languages	More languages	Study languages	Interfacing
Limited perception	Obtain full perception	Travel mountain tops	Trust

Table 1.

Naïve or interesting, we'll come back to these results later.
Very limited desk top search
Type "common glossary" in exact wording at Google
Get 46,100 hits.
Type "common glossary information" in exact wording at Google
Get none.
Type "information glossary" in exact wording at Google
Get 114,000 hits.
Type "information security glossary" in exact wording at Google
Get 17,200 hits.
Going to some of these hits I found the following:

3. A definition of Information Security

"The process of protecting data from accidental or intentional misuse by persons inside or outside of an organization. Although information security is by no means strictly a technical problem, its technical aspects (firewalls, encryption and the like) are important. Information security is an increasingly high-profile problem, as hackers take advantage of the fact that more organizations are opening parts of their systems to employees, customers and other businesses via the Internet."
www.csoonline.com/glossary

The European Network and Information Security Agency, (Heraklion, Greece) is co-organizing the biggest non-commercial, strategic conference in Europe on Network and Information Security, the annual ISSE (Information Security Solutions Europe) taking place for the 8th consecutive year.

This year, the conference is located in Rome from October 10-12 2006.
http://www.enisa.eu.int/pages/01_01.htm
http://www.enisa.eu.int/index.htm

Information security can, of course, be made difficult to interpret and understand due to the overuse of jargon and technical terminology. The ISO 17799 Toolkit therefore includes an item to specifically address this problem.

The 'Information Security Glossary' is a core part of the product. It explains each of many hundreds of technical terms and phrases in simple every day language.
The jargon is NOT made even worse by using jargon to explain it!

This outstanding item is intended for use, not just when addressing the ISO 17799 standard, but within the IT and security arena generally.

http://www.17799-toolkit.com/17799glos.htm

Also the following links were interesting for me:

http://www.alphadictionary.com/directory/Specialty_Dictionaries/Security/

http://www.isd.salford.ac.uk/governance/security/infosechand.pdf#search=%22%20%22information%20security%20glossary%22%22

http://www.security-manual.com/glos.htm

http://www.information-security-policies-and-standards.com/

Despite the many interesting discoveries, in conclusion of my very limited desk top study I must ask: "what is new here?" as the first impressions lead to the "as always" conclusions:

Private companies are in the lead?!

Yet the European Union is rather active with its European Network and Information Security Agency and its i2010 Action Plan;

Super focus on hardware and software; limited focus on the Human Factor?!

Yet is seems that the Human Factor is winning grounds via more spread theories and movements from the inside;

Too much single focus in stead of multi-disciplinary focus?!

Yet the awareness for process- and chain orientation seems emerging.

4. Intermediate conclusions

There is no C-VIS at the level of satisfactory usability for NATO Russia Council Science Committee; or

There is no C-VIS at the level of satisfactory usability for NATO and Russia; or

There is no C-VIS at the level of satisfactory usability for governments and supra/international entities in the security area; or

There is no C-VIS at the level of satisfactory usability for entities in the security area.

Worst case scenario here is the last option, which I estimate may be true, due to the level of co-operation within and between law enforcement and criminal justice bodies, let alone the security services. In case of applicability of the first option the crisis is serious though, related to its 3.5 years existence, limited. In this case I would anyway suggest to adaptively link up to existing models and mechanisms, however us being here explains that this is easier said than done, and perhaps just for the simple reason that this scenario is being dwarfed by the worst case scenario.

5. Need for further definition

Obviously I'm puzzled and my views on C-VIS get blurred: I need focus.

Are we discussing *the* common glossary?

And then: whose commonality?

And then also: on information, on security, on both or *just* on information security?

Besides, when common vocabularies in the information security area exist, what do and what should they cover?

Safety and security to their widest possible extend or just information and/or information security related topics?

Talking its glossary: what is information security?
Above, we read: "The process of protecting data from accidental or intentional misuse by persons inside or outside of an organization."
"What are data?" is an inevitable question here, but I believe it is also interesting to see its context:

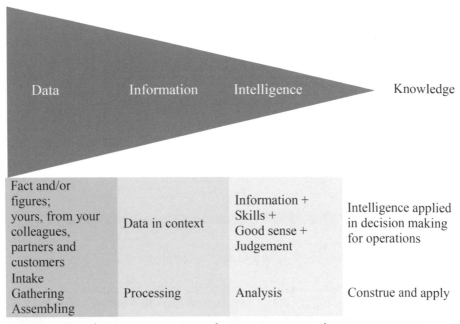

Data	Information	Intelligence	Knowledge
Fact and/or figures; yours, from your colleagues, partners and customers	Data in context	Information + Skills + Good sense + Judgement	Intelligence applied in decision making for operations
Intake Gathering Assembling	Processing	Analysis	Construe and apply

<<<<<<<<<<<improve<<<<<<<<evaluate<<<<<<<<monitor<<<<<<<<<<<<

Fig. 2.

This matter seems to encompass everything and everybody, isn't it?
This brings me to the following two viewpoints:
From a theoretical viewpoint, security can be organized on every acre. However, a totalitarian police state would come free of charge, implying people not feeling free with that.
From the same theoretical viewpoint, freedom can be organized on every acre. Then, a perverted, depraved society would come free of charge, implying people not feeling secure with that.
Are we to balance freedom and security? I do not believe so, as these are not really counterbalances.
Are we to technocratically regulate freedom and security? I do not believe so, as we cannot robotize human life.
I believe we are to orchestrate legislation, policy, structures, management and operations; something like orchestrating life, orchestrating society? Yes, orchestrating all of us, incorporating and advocating the ideals of freedom and security. Not just mine, but ours.

And this implies false tunes every now and then.
So, we're back again to another basic: reducing risks.
C-VIS is all about reducing risks.

6. Some figures

IT-professionals claimed it was them who took down the Berlin Wall, prior to the actual opening at November 9 1989 at 10.30 p.m., as they made it possible for information to pass the barrier without a problem.
IT and www. connected the world:

Regional Groupings[2] Country	Numbers in Millions						%Change	
	1991	1992	1993	1994	1995	1996	1991-1996	2000[3]
North America	66.57	73.70	83.30	94.00	106.00	118.97	78.7%	182.10
European Union	31.70	37.52	44.24	51.71	60.08	69.89	120.5%	131.67
European Free Trade Assoc.	1.26	1.52	1.78	2.14	2.50	3.00	138.1%	5.50
Central and Eastern Europe	1.24	1.69	2.25	2.90	3.69	4.74	282.0%	7.43
Asia-Pacific	16.28	20.18	24.89	30.89	39.02	48.55	198.2%	10.83
Latin America	1.68	2.31	3.15	4.17	5.40	6.84	307.1%	15.56
Worldwide Totals	136.90	159.20	186.90	218.80	257.20	301.00	119.9%	557.00

Table 2. Number of Computers In Use 1991-2000

BBC News read December 15th 2004:
"The number of personal computers worldwide is expected to double by 2010 to 1.3 billion machines, according to a report by analysts Forrester Research. The growth will be driven by emerging markets such as China, Russia and India. More than a third of all new PCs will be in these markets, with China adding 178 million new PCs by 2010. Low-priced computers made by local companies are expected to dominate in such territories. There are currently 575 million PCs in use globally. The United States, Europe and Asia-Pacific are expected to add 150 million new PCs by 2010.The report forecast that there will be 80 million new PC users in India by 2010 and 40 million new users in Indonesia."

---

[2] Regional Groupings
North America = Canada, Mexico and United States
European Union = Austria, Belgium, Denmark, Finland, Germany, Ireland, Italy, The Netherlands, Portugal, Spain, Sweden, and the United Kingdom (excludes Luxemburg)
European Free Trade Association = Norway and Switzerland (excludes Iceland)
Central and Eastern Europe = Bulgaria, Czech Republic, Hungary, Poland, Slovakia and Ukraine
Asia-Pacific = Australia, China, Hong Kong, India, Indonesia, Japan, Malaysia, New Zealand, Philippines, Singapore, South Korea, Taiwan and Thailand
Latin America = Argentina, Brazil, Chile, Colombia, Peru, and Venezuela
[3] Projected
Source: Computer Industry Almanac, Inc.
Excerpt from AEA Report Cybernation. For more information see www.aeanet.org

According to the International Programs Center, U.S. Bureau of the Census, the total population of the World, projected to 09/18/06 at 10:54 GMT (EST+5) is 6,544,841,859.[4]

575 million PC's (end 2004 information) imply at least 1 PC per 10 people.

7. Questions

How come that the United States of America were able to realize their prisoners flights throughout Europe? Was this information secured technically? Many people were involved as well, so how come they did not speak or leak? Did not they speak or leak? Most certainly the weakest link in information security is man.
How come that many information security process function?
Most likely due to a code combined with a culture.

8. Focus

In that perspective, I believe it is wise to focus on codes and cultures, and that brings me back to my crisis-grid:

Crisis	Inversed	Reasonable Action	Next best RA
Not scientist	Scientist	Study science	Dialogue
30 years police	30 years no police	Reflect and assist	
Dutch	De-Dutch	Travel the world	Read
Only 5 languages	More languages	Study languages	Interfacing
Limited perception	Obtain full perception	Travel mountain tops	Trust

Table 3.

Most of the reasonable actions mentioned are tiresome for me:
I do not have enough energy to start studying and become an academic as well;
I have perhaps not even seen 5 % of the world
Study another language is alluring, but too time consuming;
I do travel mountain tops, but far too little, as I allocate insufficient time to do so: my time-management needs improvement.
The next best reasonable options are not only easier doable, also nicer:
I like dialogues, as they connect to the obvious and the unexpected, including science;
I already reflected and assisted being a police – officer, but even being positively critical faced dismissal various times due to alleged insubordination; the last 7 years I am "on the outside" and continue to the best of my capacities reflecting and assisting however from a broader vision and mission, which is attractive: it opens your mind and gives new insights;
I do travel a lot for my work and also privately I'm interested in differing cultures; if time and budget do not allow travel, I read;

---

[4] Source: http://start.csail.mit.edu/startfarm.cgi?query=How+many+people+live+on+Earth%3F

Use the default as interface, make yourself vulnerable, and ask for help from interfaces: I have more times been helped than left alone;
As I cannot do everything myself, I rely on people, I trust people.[5]

Doing so, we might be open for thoughts and discussion on all blind spots; we might enlighten ourselves; through dialogue and exchanges of good and poor experiences we might even enlighten others; in the end we might even use more of the capacities given to us by nature.

9. Solution?

I hope my message is clear. Alongside all technical provisions, we need to have an equal strong focus on the soft side, on the Human Factor. Also here, the effect of the action is always the product of its quality and its acceptance. ($E = A \times Q$)

It helps if we not only think & act products, but also think & act processes.
Any programme, project or action, so also C-VIS, should be designed, implemented and evaluated round the three following themes:
Binding agreements on quality and methodology;
Clearly defined and performed roles and responsibilities, both horizontally and vertically (hierarchically);
Continuous improvement mechanisms.

Preconditioned here are the following three organizational settings:
Recruitment, training and education, continued validation and certification of craftsmanship of people involved;
Gradual shift from management to leadership in all three stages of design, implementation and evaluation;
Organizational focus on cultural aspects of co-operation, including the integration of a culture of dissent;

In our efforts on improving information security, we could also use the powers "from the inside": improve information security as an automatic result from improved information and intelligence processes.
Based on the model of the European Foundation for Quality Management, a model for progressive organizational maturation, the Dutch scientist Ir. W.J.C. Luiten[6] developed a matrix.[7]

The use of the matrix offers insights on your organizational state of play as well as on the rationale for improvement. Intrinsically, following the growth of your organization, you bring people together, performing from a more common setting. People creating a mutual working culture, sharing common codes.

---

[5] Please note: if you fool me, you are to blame; if you fool me twice, I am to blame

[6] 'Excellente informatie-voorziening', Informatievoorziening die bijdraagt aan de realisatie van uw organisatiedoelen, IR. W.J.C. Luiten, pp 31, translated: Excellent information services, Information services contributing to the realisation of your corporate objectives

[7] Although there is one clear weak spot, indeed, no particular *chapter* on information security, the concept at least is worth consideration

Phase & Orientation	Phase I – Activity	Phase II – Process	Phase III – System	Phase IV – Chain	Phase V – Transformation
General picture	Information services based on personal initiative. Information will be used as far as there is a craftsmanship based need. Possibly ICT is used.	Information services are aiming at improving and optimization of primary processes. ICT is focused entirely on implementation and management of primary processes. Sub optimization quite often is inevitable.	Information services are intentionally deployed and utilized by the organization to manage all processes. This implies not only implementation of and support to primary (production) processes, but also for the benefits of the management of the organization. External information is gathered to manage pro-actively. ICT is a tool to connect and combine processes and to execute integral management.	Information services are intentionally deployed to support the entire chain. Information services connect and combine primary (production) processes throughout the entire chain and support tuning and harmonization of organizational management.	Information services not only support the own organization and its chain, but gives impulses tom possible transformations. Information is gathered structurally, allowing exploration of possible transformations and design and calculation of subsequent scenarios.
Strategy and information policy Starting points on how to use information services within the organization Harmonization	No accepted information strategy exists; no criteria exist, neither basic principle. Accepted preconditions are unknown. Information strategy	First steps towards an information strategy, exclusively focusing on the primary process.	Information strategy and policy are an integral part of the business strategy and policy. The benefits of information services are clear.	Strategy and policy of the organizations own information services are tuned to and harmonized with information services of partners in the chain.	Future scenarios determine information services policy. Information strategy and policy are an example for other organizations.

Table 4.

Phase & Orientation	Phase I – Activity	Phase II – Process	Phase III – System	Phase IV – Chain	Phase V – Transformation
between the organization and information services. (Business / IT Alignment)	and policy are a non priority.		Information strategy is based on customers needs. Information strategy and policy are being evaluated. Management of innovation in information services exists.	Information services are deployed to re-enforce the entire chain together with the partners. Information services' PDCA-cycle is complete. New projects and activities are based on achievements.	
Infrastructure Mainframes, servers, PC's/laptops, printers, modems, routers, cabling, satellites, etcetera	The information infrastructure is historically grown, and is not the result of a conscious choice. No standards exist. Usually stand alone systems.	The infrastructure is derived from the primary process. Incidentally department / division transcending links exist.	Information infrastructure is tuned to and supports integral management. All employees have the necessary ICT available.	Optimization of infrastructure in co-operation with chain partners.	Information infrastructure is developed in co-operation with external partners and environment. It is authoritative and a model. Knowledge and insights are available for others.
Organization of information services Co-ordination of policy, system-application- and information management, helpdesk	Ad-hocracies, information services are not organized according roles, responsibilities and competences.	Management of the existing focused on the primary process, keeping it alive. The ICT-organization distinguishes specialized functions.	Information services are part of integral line-management at all levels.	Information services entities of all organization sin the chain co-operate according the PDCA-cycle.	The organization of information services commits itself to strategic alliances for the future.

Table 4. (Continued.)

Phase & Orientation	Phase I – Activity	Phase II – Process	Phase III – System	Phase IV – Chain	Phase V – Transformation
Data and information Data, information, intelligence, knowledge, what is it used for?	Registration is focused on being held accountable, particularly in the financial domain and very disintegrated recorded.	Data from the primary process are the basis for its management; also financial data are available. Privacy and security are organized.	Data are used for integral management. Project management is explicitly supported by information services. Data are recorded once-only for multiple use (data warehousing) Information becomes knowledge	Information services are organized from the chain perspective. Reliability and integrity of employees are beyond questioning.	Management-information is available for benchmarking
Software Operating software, office automation, special applications	A mishmash of software, facilitating registration of activities	Software is facilitating processing of transactions in the primary process. Interfaces emerge.	Transaction-information becomes management information. Enterprise Resource Planning really works. Applications and management are integrated throughout the organization.	Software concurs with — de facto — standards in the chain	One contributes to the development of standards for the benefits of one's own excellence and others' excellence.

Table 4. (Continued.)

I advocate a stronger focus on Human Capital and their values and this is also elucidated by others.

In "De economische waarde van werknemers" [8] one can read:
"In many organizations it is a habitual ritual: at the end of the year, gathered for the distribution ceremony of the Christmas Boxes, or during the New Years Reception, the CEO heartening his or her employees with *'pep talk'*: 'Our staff is our most valuable capital good' is often heard.

However, during the rest of the year, staffs are not seen as an *asset*, but as *'costs walking about on legs'*. This is also caused by the fact that managers do not have adequate insight in the creation of value by their staff. Current bookkeeping approach displays the costs of staff, not the profits."

"Staff is an *'intangible asset'* and no economic property. However for the success of organizations it is a very essential and substantial *asset*. Leading authors and management gurus therefore correctly pay much attention to the 'human factor'."

"In order to understand how final financial results of an organization are realized, one needs to acquire understanding of the role and purpose of:
The quality of the organization and its staff and their development in terms of learning and growing;
The effectiveness and efficiency of internal corporate processes;
Customer satisfaction and loyalty."

"As Kaplan and Norton argue, motivation and competences of employees are essential. The focus on *shareholders value* and corresponding accountability mechanisms often lead to a policy in which the optimization term dos not exceed 'tomorrow 12.00 hours'.
In realizing future profits from a continuity-perspective, one needs to pay sufficient attention to the further development of key competences."

"The alignment of human capital and information capital with strategic internal processes is essential. The era of continuous change, shorter product-life-cycles and the need for faster 'time to market' makes the art of mobilization of these assets to support strategic changes essential to realize changes and adjustments. This requires a good and flexible working force, which is employable and innovative by nature. Human capital, as *'intangible asset'*, can make the difference between survival and meeting with disaster."

Next to the human individual, it's an open door to refer to co-operation. The more this seems easy and natural, the more we all know this is rather difficult and certainly not always experienced as obvious.
"Samenspelen is ook een kwaliteit."[9]

"...the successful communication of values to your employees or, in other words, the steering of staff without direct control, will be companies' critical success factor"

---

[8] Translated: "Economic value of employees". Thesis, in short pronounced at the occasion of the public assumption of the office of Professor of Human Capital Valuation at the Tilburg University, June 4th 2004, Prof. dr. Gerard H.M. Evers, Universiteit van Tilburg, Faculteit der Sociale Wetenschappen, IVA beleidsonderzoek en advies, 2004, pp 44, ISBN 90-6835-399-3
[9] Translated: "Playing together is also a quality" Marco van Basten, coach of the Dutch National Soccer Team, during a press conference, Lausanne, May 24th 2006

Before 1900	Official	ROS, return on sales	Volume
1900 – 1950	Industrial	ROI, return on investment	Efficiency
1950 – 1990	Thematic	ROE, return on equity	Learning together
From 1990	Networking	ROT, return on trust	Create together
From 2001	Human Capital	ROP, return on people	Joint construction and maintenance of knowledge and competences
Future	Human Values	ROV, return on values	Joint values, codes and conventions

Table 5.[10]

More and more, the product orientation gets matrixed by the process-orientation, which means that there is a stronger focus on:

Results during and achievements at the end of processes, which are key: what do all people involved realize?!

The process orientation is the leading principle, the co-existence of processes is not enough, they must inter-act and they must match!

Creativity is one step; innovation is the next one, as innovation is applied creativity. In this perspective craftsmanship needs to be cherished, by providing them means to professionally exercise their work!

Good information services are a precondition to adjust and match working processes: the relevance of information security needs no further clarification!

A strong external orientation< from entities within one organization and from organizations amongst themselves) is the key factor to determine the success for co-operation!

The Human Factor is always the uniting link![11]

In this perspective, head-hunting is history, heart-hunting is key.[12]

10. In conclusion

Ladies and gentlemen,

Perhaps my presentation has been disappointing:

I sincerely apologies, as that implies I have not met to my customers' expectations, most likely due to a poor preparation;

---

[10] Drs. S. Bron, RA RC AA, Controller Hay Group, during the Workshop "Mensen op de Balans", (translated: People on the Scales) March 31st 2003, Hay Vision Society, Workshop paper by Selma van den Berg, Eric Verduyn, Jan-Peter Koning, pp 17

[11] Authors' free interpretation of the documents: Functie en toepassing RBP, versie 1.0, Werkgroep VPP en Projectgroep, 23 januari 2006, pp7, Referentiemodel Bedrijfsprocessen Politie, RBP 2006 *Stapsgewijze toelichting RBP 2006,* Powerpointpresentatie van Dr. M. Nieuwenhuis, Werkgroep RBP, CIP, Kwaliteitsbureau Politie, 13 dia's, RBP 2006, Referentiemodel Bedrijfsprocessen Politie, versie 3.0, Werkgroep VPP en Projectgroep VPP, 5 april 2006, pp54 documents drafted in the framework of improving the working processes of the Dutch Police

[12] See: "De HeartHunter", Value driven organisation transformation, Drs. Egbert Kinds, Management & Literatuur, edition 2, November 1st 2000

Perhaps my presentation was surprising:

I then can be relieved, as that implies I have at least provoked or stimulated your mind set;

Perhaps my presentation has been interesting:

Only then I can be satisfied, as that implies that you already are processing bits and bytes of it, for the benefits of your future actions.

And perhaps your future action results in a C-VIS which is close to being comprehensive[13], as a result from genuine mutual understanding.

A mutual understanding of which I hope it is focusing on results, directly related to improving the quality of information and not related to cover up.

As covering up cannot be brought in line with the rule of law, principles of good governance, democracy and not even human rights.

Here is my concrete suggestion of indispensable terms in C-VIS.

Thank you for your attention.

---

[13] I suggest being satisfied with about 80%, as striving for the full 100% perhaps slows down the first issuing; the 20 remaining %'s can de dealt with during the first and following improvement cycles

A Process for Developing a Common Vocabulary in the Information Security Area
J. von Knop et al. (Eds.)
IOS Press, 2007

About Information Concept, Its Essence, and Role in Social and Technical Systems

Prof. Dr. Alexandr V. FEDOROV
Foreign Affairs Academy, Moscow

The given material has for the most part theoretical nature and is devoted to analysis of existing in social science approaches[1] to understanding and social role of such phenomenon as information.

It is generally accepted that the next level of society development will be (or already is) "information society" in which information becomes (or is supposed to become) an efficient power and a main subject of labor. However, there is no common understanding of this term. But without clarity in this issue it is difficult to discuss not only finding solutions but even the legitimacy of stating applied problems in the field of information relations. Naturally, these issues also include objectives for information society development and providing information security. This is why any research of political and legal aspects of providing international information security should begin with finding a definition for term "information" and its derivatives.

1. The Concept of Information

The term "information" comes from Latin word "informatio" that means inquiry, exposition, or explanation. An everyday perception of information represents messages and data with certain content. Defining dictionaries distinguish such meaning of information as findings, news, data, and knowledge obtained through research and observation, including facts prepared for messaging. But generally definition of the term information remains on intuitional level. The law of the Russian Federation "About Information, Information Technolgies, and Information Protection" (passed by the State Duma of the Federal Assembly of the Russian Federation on July 8, 2006) defines information as "findings (messages, data) regardless of their representation form" (Article 2). The text does not clarify the terms "findings (messages, data)". Therefore it is not clear if any message (data) is information.

Journalism made attempts to conduct a scientific research of information phenomenon starting in 20-s of the 20th century. Basing on the popular interpretation in this field of information as a description of facts, first researchers discussed if any or only new facts should be considered as information. They classified information sources, studied relationship between a consumer (a newspaper reader) and information itself, conditions of its perception, and properties of public significant information

---

[1] The detailed analysis of such approaches and theoretical concepts are stated in Fedorov A.V. "International Information Security in World Political Process" Moscow, Moscow State Institute (University) for International Relations, 2006.

including reliability, importance, completeness, and credibility[2]. The important role of information in politics and its influence on public morality are distinguished in a number of international documents of the last century[3]. However, the information phenomenon became a topic for active scientific discussions only in the second half of the 20th century. The reason for that was a theoretical development stimulated by telecommunication demand and creation of computing machines, which were also used for military purposes. The results of research conducted by C.Shennon[4], who has used methods of probability theory for measuring information quantity, transmitted through communication lines, and for defining means for optimal encryption, have influenced a lot the development of information theory. However Shennon did not give a definition for the term information itself.

K.Viner's study contributed to forming "information view" on customary and newly designed objects. First attempts made by N.Viner and his followers to use ideas of information and cybernetics theory in anthropological and social reflexion, on the one side, created impulse for further serious research of information properties and role in systems of certain type and, on the other side, stimulated general research that studies information specifics in different fields.

Emergence and wide spread of personal computers, available for every non-professional user and especially Internet that became an information technological symbol in the beginning of the new century, encouraged elevation of public attention to information processing and usage, to issues of information policy and strategy.

In this case it is logical that social political ideas related to understanding of information society became popular. The basis for this theory was established in Japan in the end of 60's – beginning of 70's with not generally known concept that assumed escalation of "information capacity" of manufacturing goods due to increase of their value through innovations, design, marketing, and transformation of informational (not material) product manufacturing into driving force of society formation and development[5]. Thereafter a specific convergence of information society ideas with ideas of post-industrialism has occurred. The classical version of post-industrialism is presented in studies of the American sociologist Daniel Bell, who endued knowledge and information with "strategic resource" and "determinative variables" status. He believed that knowledge and information would replace such "determinative variables of the industrial society" as labor and capital[6]. Characteristics of the information society distinguished by current Russian researchers conform Bell's ideas. The information society is defined as a "society based on knowledge", where individuals and groups are provided with access to information and knowledge vital for everyday activity and for solving private and social issues[7]. Nowadays postmodern

---

[2] See Afanasev V.G., Ursul A.D. Social Information. (Some Methodological aspects) // Philosophy Matters. 1974. # 10, p. 61-62

[3] Collection of Main Documents and Materials related to International Relations in the field of Information. Moscow, Ministry of Foreign Affairs, 1984

[4] Shannon C. A Mathematical Theory of Communication // Bell System Techno. J., 27 (1948), No 3, 27 (1948), No.4

[5] See Masuda Y. *The Information Society as Postindustrial Society.* Wash.: World Future Soc., 1983, p. 29

[6] Bell D. *The Social Framework of the Information Society.* Oxford, 1980.

[7] See: Rakitov A.I. *Philosophy of Computer Revolution.* Moscow. Politizdat. 1991; Ershova T.V. *Conceptual Matters of Transition to Information Society of the XXI Century.* // Herald Russian Foundation for Basic Research (RFBR). #3. September 1999; Meluhin I.S. *Information Society.* Moscow. MSU Publisher House. 1999

interpretations become popular[8]. According to postmodern theory information society perspectives are closely related to increasing non-scientific role of information and "scientific discourse loss of its privileged status". Information society faces an increasing possibility of unreliable information, disinformation or such forms of information presentation that disable message evaluation as true or false dissemination. Control automation in technical systems, including military systems, lead to these statements. Control automation systems are based on the same methods and technical procedures as human processing of "intellectually relevant" information. What is the difference between the "Enter" button and button or buttons (missile systems have two buttons) of electric impulse that activates trigger mechanism of artillery or missile launching system from the result perspective? Virtually, it is the same command; therefore, it is also an information message. A complex of electric, electromagnetic, wave, or flash impulses should be examined in different networks including computer communication lines and information networks. Clearly, even in the simplest conversation information between sources of vocal apparatus (speaker) and consumers acoustic apparatus (listener) exists as a sonic acoustic wave. Thus, it would be wrong to relate information only to human consciousness. This is the reason why those who deal with information as a phenomenon believe that it is necessary to place not only information and human consciousness in infosphere but everything related to information, information transmission systems, information receiving and storage including person, society, individual and public consciousness, public relations dealing with information, and information infrastructures[9]. That is to say the whole complex of information, systems of its storage and processing, and all possible channels for information impact on individual and social technical systems.

What is an information phenomenon? On the one hand, the wide use of this term, an implication of new contexts lead to homonymy, meaning that the word "information" is understood differently and it obtains various meanings. On the other hand, a philosophical understanding of information nature, the comparison of different approaches to information study, and the exposure of advantages and boundaries for using the given term become crucial.

2. Main Explications of the Term

Without giving a detailed analysis of all know explications of the term information[10], basing on interpretation of information as messages irrespectively from source, receiver, and transmission mode, the following closely related to D.Bell's and K.Shenon's approaches definition of information can be given.
Information:

---

[8] One of the representatives of such an approach is one of the Bell's critics an American sociologist M.Poster who offers his own concept of "information mode" similarly to the K.Marx's concept of "production mode". See: Poster M. The Mode of Information: Poststructuralism and Social Context. Cambridge: Polity Press, 1990

[9] Streltsov A.A. Providing Information Security in Russia. Moscow. 2002. p. 78-79

[10] Different meanings of the term are given in Streltsov A.A., Fedorov A.V. studies and glossaries included in Fedorov A.V., Zigichko V.N. (ed.) "Informational Challenges to National and International Security" (Moscow: Pir-Center, 2001) and Dictionary of Terms and Definitions in the Field of Information Security. Moscow, General Staff of the Russian Armed Forces, 2004.As far as Western terminology publication, one should pay attention to a considered official supplement for military and defense trend electronic dictionary of the U.S. DoD

1) message inseparably related to control; signals in unity of syntactic, semantic, and pragmatic characteristics;

2) transmission, reflection of variety in any objects and processes (of inanimate and animated nature);

3) data about individuals, objects, facts, events, phenomenon, and processes regardless of presentation form.

The same definition can be given as a more exact formulation which will be synonymous but less usable for practical study. However, following the scientific principles, it should be mentioned. Thus, **"under the term of information we should understand a reflection of processes, phenomena, or certain events of inanimate and animated nature in objects of physical world regardless of reflections form, carrier, and position in time and space."**

These definitions (or one definition because as it was mentioned above the author considers the definitions to be synonyms), on the one hand, correspond to technological approach because as C. Shennon has put it "the main objective of communication involves precise or proximate reproduction of message in some place, which was chosen for its transmission in other place"[11]. From this point of view a written or typed sentence telling about some event is considered to be a sequence of symbols that are being encrypted in signals. This sentence is not different from chain of electric impulses in modern automation control systems of industrial enterprise, weapon systems, nuclear power plant, hydroelectric power plant, satellite communication systems, or any other modern industrial or operating complex. On the other hand, the content influence remains and the information in human communication acts as basis for subjects' communicativeness.

The duality of such approach is defined by potential informational vulnerability and threat environment. Information security deals with minimization of a number of these threats. Information (technical) systems and communication systems as well as people who are engaged in the process of information obtaining and processing, act as objects for informational vulnerability.

This is of crucial importance. The pragmatic information concepts tend either to take into account technical aspects of the information processing system, bringing information threats to threats of information transmission and processing, or to its "human" aspect absolutising in particular such conceptions as information value and benefit for its owner. Moreover, "information is valuable because it helps to achieve a set goal. The same information can have different value for achieving different goals"[12]. And the theoretic of information warfare studies information in this respect: if it is an individual who is a targeted object, then information is considered as a tool for conducting a psychological attack. If the targeted objects are the communication and control systems, then information turns into electromagnetic pulse and transmission of this pulse to channels of communication and control system leads to systems failure, including changing of transmitted messages and, therefore, transformation of control action.

Virtually at the bottom of this definition lies an approach to information as to a reflective variety and to information process as to reflection of variety, as it was suggested by Russian philosophers A.D.Ursul and B.V. Birukov[13] in 70's, basing on

---

[11] Shannon K. Studies on Theory of Information and Cybernetics. Moscow. Publishing House of Foreign Literature. 1963. p. 243-244

[12] Harkevich A.A. *About Information Value //* Cybernetics Issues. 1960. # 4, p.54

[13] See: Control. Information. Intellect. A.I.Berg and other. Moscow. Misl. 1976. p.187

W.Ashby's variety concept, who used materials of statistical information theory (Ashby claimed that information theory studies processes of "variety transmission" through communication channels but quantity of information can not be transmitted in larger amounts than variety permits). Setting aside a question of communication channels, through which the information is being transmitted, philosophers concentrated on object-carrier of transmitted variety ("reflected object") and object that receives the variety ("reflecting object" that receives, perceives variety). This "variety reflected" understanding of information is being developed by these and other authors[14] and in some way it is close to mentioned above common understanding of information as data that reflects variety. It does not contradict existing information theories and presumes certain analogies with them. The reflection concept in this case goes beyond the cognitive theory limits and acts as an ontological category. This is not a question of cognizable object reflection in consciousness of cognizing subject but a question of any changes in elements, connections or functional peculiarities of one object that correspond to similar changes in another object. The followers of this approach believe that one of its main advantages is that it opens opportunities for "obtaining" information in nature systems including differentiation of informational form of causality[15].

In this context projection of general approach to given studies and limitation of this projection with research are, probably, justified for practical application. In particularly, as far as legal matters, we need to agree with O.A.Gorodov's thesis that "an issue of forming definition of information in legal science should be solved according to understanding of this phenomenon in other sciences and by using categorical concepts of law. Such categorical concept is an object of legal relations"[16]. However, it should be taken into account that absolutization on such approach leads other authors to conclusions that significantly limit the definition of information itself and its use beyond legal context. Thus, for establishment of legal relation (this can be done only between legal entities which are individuals and their associations) in the field of information it is often suggested "to consider information as a reflection result of material world objects motion in animate nature systems and in human organism in particularly"[17]. In this case data contained in technical systems (electronic data banks, information network sites, messages, circulating in communication lines, etc.), data that exists as sound waves, electric or electromagnetic pulses, or other expressions of physical processes that exist beyond human consciousness, is considered only as information carrier and qualifies for legal relations only in this quality. By all means, this approach has a right to exist but only under a condition of its particular issue-related use. Thus, its use for information security is very limited and it can be used in military fields only for conducting informational psychological operations.

At the same time a lack of general definition for information (the mentioned above definition was given by the author definition and it is not widely used yet) which can unite all other interpretations of information as particular cases (meaning interpretations for practical use), does not mean that different concepts of information

---

[14] See: Rakitov A.I. *Philosophy of Computer Revolution*. Moscow. Politizdat. 1991

[15] See: Ukraintsev B.S. Reflection in Inanimate Nature. Moscow. 1969. Informational Form of Causality // Philosophical Basics for Natural Science. Moscow. 1976

[16] Gorodov O.A. Principles of Information Law in Russia. Saint-Petersburg. Juridicheskij Zentr Press. 2003. p.19

[17] Streltsov A.A. and others. *Development of Legal Groundwork for Information Security*. Moscow. Prestige. 2005. p.11

do not have anything in common other then the word "information". Such a conclusion would be wrong to make because ideas distinctive for some concepts and approaches partially mentioned in other concepts and approaches. Sometimes, as in case with thermodynamic and logic-semantic understanding of information, we deal with fairly strict interpretations and definitions. Due to "human" context character and specific role of philosophical categories in evaluation of experience uncertainty in pragmatic and general philosophical concepts is unavoidable.

If from epistemological point of view formalizing various results of human cognitive activity in systems of signs is considered a "reflection", then within the social philosophy (and social science theory) this process can be described as information production[18]. Other types of informational activity, which matter regardless of acceptance or denial of 'reflection" approach to information, can be distinguished. These are: transferring of meaning content from one semiotic system to another (information transfer); replay of the same information product in greater or smaller quantity (information replication); information transmission (or retransmission) with or without technical support; use of information for new information creation or for achieving new results; information storage, providing an opportunity for information update within time, including its transmission and use, which basically saying means information image on tangible medium(in social systems it is persons memory); information disruption through physical destruction of symbol base or moral elimination (disavowal) of the text, including changes in content, that exclude distortion compensation with given means, creation of technical and semiotic barriers for information transmission.

Mentioned types of informational activity of social subjects can be considered as basic, while other types of activity are understood as their combination. For example, information dissemination presumes it transmission and replications that can be conducted at the same time and appear to be a physical act regardless of the content. The given approach is related to information analysis as a basis for social communication taking into account specific character of various social subjects' activity and information peculiarities that show up differently in one or another type of activity. As a matter of fact these arguments without damaging social causality can be easily used in any other abstract system, including technical system, where elements exchange information. In this case we come to an approach, which is strictly and precisely developed in S.P.Rastorguev studies[19]. Thereby engineers activity, who controls city's life support systems, navigation service employee work, scientists (in natural or human sciences) studies, journalist or individuals activity, work of computer technologies developer and user, or any mechanical system fit well into his approach. Such topics as information reliability, credibility, and efficiency stay very relevant. At the same time situations of direct information impact (or interaction) are taken into consideration. Thus, information objectiveness as a phenomenon, which emergence in different systems (social, technical, etc.) does not mean various hypostases but only projections on these systems, is provided. This creates methodological basis for studying information as a whole and in its particular exposures, for studying relations between different subjects, and objects of the material world in relation to information interaction.

---

[18] The given distinction between different types of informational activity is based on classification presented B.A.Grushin studies.
[19] Rastorguev S.P. Information Warfare. Moscow. 1998. Philosophy of Information Warfare, Moscow. 2001. Introduction into Formal Theory of Information Warfare. Moscow. 2002, etc.

Different models of information and information communication can be used in chosen context, depending on studied problem and research objectives. These can be not only "transmissive models" that contain C. Shennon's scheme of one-way communication "information source – transmitter – communication line - receiver – addressee" as a basis but they can be interaction models that consider changes in "infofund" of all their communicators[20].

---

[20] In this case the term "infofund" is used according to V.Z.Kogan study "A Human in Information Flow"(Novosibirsk. "Nauka". 1981), who has analyzed communication as a mutual impact of subjects on information aggregation (infofund), that every subject posses. Here we can see a parallel to S.P.Rastorguev's approach: communicators act as self-learning systems and they change their information reservoir in interaction process.

A Process for Developing a Common Vocabulary in the Information Security Area
J. von Knop et al. (Eds.)
IOS Press, 2007

Terms for the Glossary on Counter Cyberterrorism

Prof. Dr. Valery A. VASENIN and Dr. Oleg V. KAZARIN
Information Security Institute, Lomonosov University, Moscow

Abstract. This report analyzes the phenomenon of cyberterrorism, as well as linguistic, semantic and technical notions in the field of hi-tech terrorism and counteraction to it. Some of these notions and definitions can be included in the multilingual glossary on information security.

Introduction

The threat of using hi-technology for terrorist purposes and *the cyberterrorist threat* in particular, are among the most dangerous. As in investigation of any natural phenomenon, technical object, or phenomenon in the realm of social relations, the efficiency and final result are mostly defined by the initial system of ideas or "coordinates" of the space in which the subject under research is being analyzed. The primary goals of this report are:

- formulating the fundamentals, which help systematize and form approaches to computer terrorism research;
- developing basic concepts in the field of counter-cyberterrorism;
- developing an interrelated, scientifically proven, set of terms and definitions in the field of counter-cyberterrorism.

The starting point in analyzing any object is giving a *definition* to the object. Depending upon the researchers' goals, experiences, notions, and concepts, the definition of the object is an accumulation of the characteristics which manifest themselves in interaction with the environment. *Terrorism* is a complex, multi-faceted phenomenon. Its investigation, search of methods, and means of counteracting it, are being conducted on an inter-disciplinary level, including sociology and psychology, as well as political, judicial, and technical sciences. Correspondingly, the research model for each of the above mentioned directions will have specifics of its own. Therefore, *in the context of this particular work*, as the basic definition, unifying many characteristics of terrorism, we will use the following:

"Terrorism is **the manifestation of extremism through actions, based on disagreements (national, transnational) between separate groups of individuals with government interests and institutions (political, social, on a religious or criminal basis). Its aim is to create in the society an atmosphere of fear and tension, to form the factors which directly or indirectly destabilize national security with the goal of making demands that cannot be met in the framework of the existing regulatory field."**

We would like to mention that the above definition of terrorism does not, in the broad sense, contradict the definition given in the March 2006 federal law #35-F3, "On Counter Terrorism". However, here we significantly narrow the object of the research.   We will only focus on objects of critical infrastructure of the Russian Federation as objects of terrorist impact.

Therefore, in the basis of terrorism there lies, as a rule, political[1], religious, ethnic, social, or personal motivation based upon disagreements between certain individuals or groups of individuals, and government interests and institutions that support these interests.

As a result, we suggest the following definition of cyberterrorism.

"Cyberterrorism **is one of the types of terrorism, which, for achieving its goals:**
uses - as objects of destructive impact - informational-computing complexes and net segments, supporting systems that are critically important from point of view of the national security;
uses - as an impact method - hardware and software."

In this connection it is necessary to distinguish systems that contain information computing and telecommunication resources (data, technologies, technical means) as independent critical objects of an infrastructure in the national economic complex.

Thus, the primary goal of the cyber-terrorist attack, in the context of this report, is the critical object (CO), but the impact on it is realized through the computer system that manages the CO. So, one can single out critical objects of the national information-telecommunication infrastructure (in a broader sense – informational) which will be called *critical information objects* (CIO).

The amount of potential loss in nationally significant spheres of the economic complex can be imagined if one takes into consideration the consequences of the incidents that occurred in 2003. The short term electrical power supply interruption in some large regions of the U.S. and Canada, and the air cargo handling disruption in England, caused damage in hundreds of millions of dollars, and the resultant level of social tension influenced the political situations in the countries involved.   Similar examples in Russia are mass incidents in the system of the Russian Joint-Stock Power and Electrification Company RAO "UES" in 2005 involving four areas of Central Federal region.

"By *CO*, we mean an *object*, which in the case of partial degradation or complete loss of functions, is capable of directly, and during a relatively short period of time, influencing the state of national security, or some of its components such as management of electric power resources (nuclear, hydro), defense systems, critical industries, transport streams (railroads, aviation), information streams of government systems which support interaction of different departments."

One of the state's main objectives in the context of assuring society's interests in the field of information is to protect technologies, means and methods of processing and transmitting information messages that in many respects define, in the modern world, development of other basic spheres of public life – industrial, political, social, and spiritual.

Means and methods of information message processing and transmitting at the present level of computer engineering and telecommunication development are realized in the form of separate computing units, in network infrastructure, which provides

---

[1] Note: The given definition does not contradict, in the broad sense of the word, the definition given in the Federal Law of the Russian Federation of 06 March 2006 "On Counteracting Cyberterrorism". However, we would like to remind, that in our case, the objects protected from cyberterrorist attacks are only critically important objects.

effective unification of the units' resources and creation of large distributed complexes able to solve practically significant problems in all the above mentioned spheres of human activity basing on RAD Data Commutation technology. Assuring stable and functionally effective work of these complexes is an objective and a target of information technology security, which is a part of general information security. Along with a large number of issues solved here, the state is mostly interested in providing security to critical elements which are called "the critical elements (segments) of information infrastructure".

Such objects, significant from the point of view of national security, become targets for destructive impact in situations that can be defined as critical. These situations, first of all, include information warfare (cyber wars) as large scale actions using computer attacks and cyberterrorism that uses the same actions but for different purposes. Without going into the details of the above mentioned actions, one should notice that the top priority objectives of national security are:

- protection of the basic (backbone) elements in the telecommunication infrastructure of the Russian Federation from internal and external threats that emerge because of objective tendencies of globalization and integration processes associated with information society formation;
- creation and permanent development of security systems of information-computing and telecommunication structures that support vital functions of economic subjects critically important for state interests.

Effective realization of these objectives is impossible without scientifically grounded regulations that will allow us to effectively, and logically identify the objects of critical infrastructure, to distinguish such objects, to prescribe special conditions for their exploitation, to develop and apply means for counteracting threats that these objects are facing.

1. Basic concepts in the field of cyberterrorism and counteraction to it

1.1. Short introduction to the area of study

The character of new strategically significant threats to information security, including computer terrorism, computer crime and information warfare, generates a need to change the principles and approaches to forming and implementing security policy for information systems and nets. First, such policy should be directed to secure the function of information and telecommunication control systems for critical infrastructures. Secondly, it must decrease vulnerabilities and threats to objects, minimize the number of attacks and, if possible, their duration in order to retain the CO's controllability, and reduce the possible damage from attacks and the time for restoring the complex's function capacity. Thirdly, information security policy has to provide continuity, adequacy, and timeliness of counteraction activity of all participants (departments, establishments, organizations, and individuals that participate in this activity).

A national system of response regarding modern threats to information security has to coordinate the actions of federal authorities, local authorities of the Russian Federation, and institutions of the economic sector in organizing complex counteraction to threats to the CO: *computer crime, computer terrorism,* and *information warfare.*

In the context of this work the potential impact on such objects can be divided into two main types:

- *direct impact* (for example, physical, chemical, or biological attack) on a CO in order to disable and destroy it, including casualties among the populace;
- *impact on a CO through its control system* which is an entity of information and computing complexes and means for network support.
- The second type, which is closer to the subject of this research, can be divided into:
- *physical impact on a CO control system;*
- *impact using an electromagnetic emanation or other physical fields;*
- *impact using software that operates a CO control system.*

The last type of impact is a tool of cyberterrorism, a phenomenon that is being studied in this work.

1.2. Critical information infrastructure, critical sectors, segments, and objects

Taking into consideration the characteristics mentioned above regarding the state's vital functions in relation to the objects of critical importance and requirements of their protection from cyberterrorist threats, there is an obvious need to analyze the features (characteristics) of these objects' control systems, which are the main target (objective) for cyberterrorism. Earlier we specified the COs of national information and telecommunication infrastructure (generally understood as informational), and denoted them as COI.

In addition to the two main notions - CO and COI, the definitions of which are given above – let us have a look at some other concepts. Under *critical segments* we understand a complex of COs, united on the basis of one or several qualifying features as, for example, area of application, departmental membership, vital importance, requirements of information security and others similar to them. *Critical sector* is on a higher level of the hierarchy and characterizes a set of critical objects and/or segments related to certain sectors of national economy, national defense system, social and spiritual life.

One should bear in mind that though there are differences between such concepts as critical infrastructure (CI), critical information infrastructure (CII) or critical segments, sectors, and objects of information infrastructure on the national level, there is a close interrelation between these concepts.

Under *infrastructure* we will understand a set of separate interconnected structural elements of the system that support its functionality (assigned functioning).
Under *critical infrastructure* we will understand a set of separate, interconnected components that support functionality of Russia's vital spheres.

Under *critical information infrastructure* we will understand a complex of objects whose degradation (partial or complete) either directly or indirectly influences different aspects of national security, software, network, and information components that support Russia's national vital functions.

The given interpretation of the basic terms allows us to precisely describe identifiers of information elements and infrastructures, and to distinguish them from other notions.

2. Basic legal regulations

2.1. A phenomenon of terrorism in modern society; a concept of cyberterrorist act

Taking into consideration the statements mentioned above, we can single out *"cyberterrorism"* from the general notion of terrorism. To do this, we need to form a general concept of cyberterrorist act, a combined definition of which was studied in the article [6].

A *"cyberterrorist act"* is a motivated act conducted through computer and communication means, the usage of which can either potentially or directly cause danger to people's lives and health, can cause significant damage to material objects, dangerous consequences to society or to attract maximum attention to political demands of terrorists.

A terrorist act usually consists of two parts: *conducting the act of terrorism (violence, intimidation, material damage) and spreading the information about it's the organizers and their demands, the so-called "taking of responsibility".* With a high amount of probability, a terrorist act that is just "indicated" is conducted with minimal destructive consequences. At the same time, an information message with a threat to conduct a full scale terrorist act is presented.

The following decomposition of "cyberterrorist act" can be considered. In a narrower sense, a terrorist act will be called a cyberterrorist act if it initially uses computer software in order to damage human life and material objects. But in this case, two types of activity fall out of our view: the so-called activism and "hacktivism". Activism is dissemination of information in order to spread panic and fear among the population through legal means. Hacktivism is dissemination of the same kind of information using a hacker's methods (breaking websites and software) [6]. This activity helps to conduct the second part of the cyberterrorist act in case the first is lacking or does not correspond to the definition given above.

A broader interpretation of a cyberterrorist act includes such structural elements as activism, hacktivism and concepts related to acts that coordinate terrorist actions through use of the internet. For example, through various on-line forums and chat rooms, terrorists can exchange encrypted messages, various types of video (maps, photos, movies) and audio materials (speeches by terrorist leaders, etc.).

Besides the above activities, we can mention other activities through which terrorist organizations (using their websites, including officially registered ones) can:

- recruit and learn more about new candidates[2];
- conduct propaganda that is not under the control of government supervisory organs[3];
- disseminate information about how to manufacture weapons and explosives out of readily available products, and instructions for their use[4].

Using as a basis, the conceptual framework and informal considerations given above, in the field of general understanding of a terrorist threat in modern society and counteraction to it, we can proceed toward a stricter (more formal), scientifically

---

[2] These methods are widely used by Al Quaida (see, for example, [5])

[3] A typical example is the Chechenian separatists' web-site "Kavkaz-Center"

[4] In August 2006 O.Kostirev, I.Tihomirov, V.Dgukovzev, and N.Korolev planned and exploded a bomb on Cherkizovskij market in Moscow. As a result 12 people were killed and over 50 injured. The "recipe" for manufacturing liquid explosives was downloaded by O.Kostirev from Internet. According to certain sources, the bombers were members of an extremist organization called "Russian National Union"

grounded concept of "cyberterrorism" and notions related to it. This task is complicated due to the following reasons:

- first, the terminological base in this field is far from being developed, it is not even formed on the initial level because of departmental, sectional, disciplinary reasons, and methodological approaches of different schools;
- secondly, the subject matter itself is quite new and the cyberterrorist acts, fortunately, have not obtained a form of large scale manifestations;
- thirdly, to counteract modern destructive impacts is a difficult task, because the computer attacks conducted within the information warfare framework are considered to be computer crimes or acts of cyberterrorism, and it is very difficult to draw a line between these two concepts.

For the scientific foundation of cyberterrorism we will use a definitional approach. In practice, there are two approaches to scientific groundwork – illustrative and definitional. By illustrative method, the concept is perceived though examples; by definitional approach, though definitions [7]. Of certain importance are the legal aspects because a cyberterrorist act is regarded, naturally, as a violation of law and is a crime.

2.2. Approaches to the scientific concept of "cyberterrorism"

The problem of cyberterrorism has only recently become a matter of research. This is why the majority of leading countries, including Russia, have not yet undertaken efforts to improve legislation in this field. This situation is caused by the fact that a unified understanding of this new type of crime has not yet been formed. Such a violation of law should be formalized at the legislative level and its constituent elements should be taken into account during classification. The following elements should be examined: object, subject, aspect, and subjective aspect.

Let us look at the existing approaches and rules for determining (defining) the term "cyberterrorism". The term should meet the following requirements:

- area of the term's application (professional level of application);
- deduction; term's components logically correlated to subordinated terms and among one another (here the description of the crime is given);
- conclusion.

For a precise definition of the term studied, it should be correlated with the following terms: "terrorism", "terror", "cybernetics" and other related notions and terms that are already present in legislative practice, and their interpretations formed on the scientific and research levels.

The absence of a unified notion of "cyberterrorism" is a result of the lack of a unified methodology, or a system of principles and methods, for organizing and forming theoretical and practical activity in this field.

A systematic approach in characterizing a new term is a very important component of the identification process. The term has to take into account general legal principals, on which, the whole legal system is based, interdisciplinary (common for several disciplines) principles, and principles distinctive for particular disciplines, including information law (if it is proved that cyberterrorism is related to this type of law).

A detailed research of the existing terms and definitions of terrorism and cyberterrorism, performed by V. V. Stepanov and V. V. Starostina, was conducted within the research work "Methods and Means of Counteracting Computer Terrorism: Mechanisms, Models, Scenarios, Instruments, and Administrative and Regulatory

Solutions" (2005-BT-22.2/001). The research work was conducted within the federal task-oriented scientific technical program "Research and Development in the Priority Areas of Science and Technology Development" for 2002-2006 [6]. Without going into the details of this research, we move straight to the author's position on defining cyberterrorism and the notions related to this concept.

2.3. The author's modern interpretation (2006) of the term "cyberterrorism"

2.3.1. Primary and secondary objects of cyberterrorist impact

Synthesizing a general understanding of cyberterrorism as a phenomenon, and taking into account the above considerations, we can formulate the following definition, which will not contradict the definitions given above in a broader philosophical sense. We would like to reiterate that in the context of the previously mentioned approaches, only defense of objects of critical infrastructures will be analyzed.

Cyberterrorism[5] is a trend of terrorism that, for achieving its goals:

- uses information and computing complexes and network segments that support critically important systems from the point of view of national security, as objects of destructive impact;
- uses means of computing technology and software as subjects of impact.

In this respect we distinguish primary and secondary objects of cyberterrorist impact.

The primary object of cyberterrorist impact is generally understood as:

- computer complex for a relatively limited, but strategically important activity, able to influence human life and health, national security, and area of its application;
- large integrated system of distributed information and computing resources for serving nationally important activities (economic sector, industrial sector), [for example, energy (including nuclear), transportation (air or railroad) system and its elements (local, regional)].

The secondary objects of cyberterrorist activity are large groups of people, environment, and various material objects that can experience destructive impact to the extent of their elimination, caused by the loss of functionality by primary objects.

2.3.2. Constituent elements of "cyberterrorism" as a legal violation

Cyberterrorism as any *antisocial action* cannot be considered as a violation of the law unless its illegality is proven. The illegality is defined according to general principle.

To prove illegality of the action, the following features have to be taken into consideration:

- illegal nature of action;
- damage (casualties, social, political and other losses);
- guilt (in the case of cyberterrorism, the only form of guilt is intent, because an act of cyberterrorism cannot be conducted by inadvertence);
- ability to prove and punish a violation of the law.

Constituent elements of legal violation are a complex of established legal elements, the presence of which, allows to qualify the act as a violation of law. There four constituent elements of legal violation:

---

[5] See also comments in the introduction

- object;
- subject;
- objective aspect;
- subjective aspect.

Now we will have a closer look at each of these elements.

2.3.3. Object of cyberterrorism

The *object of a crime* (violation of law) is an element of every criminal act. This means that every crime is a criminal act only when something (social value, interest, or asset protected by criminal law) suffers, or might suffer, significant damage.

The fact mentioned is reflected in legislatively formalized feature of crime – danger to the public.

An object of a crime (including cyberterrorism) may be public relations, protected by criminal law that might suffer social damage. It is common practice in the theory of criminal law to distinguish general, special, and direct objects of a crime. In the case of cyberterrorism, the general objects will be the socio-political and economic regimes of the country. Cyberterrorism also has similar objects. The only object is public security.

If the subject of cyberterrorism does not attempt to damage public security (political or economic regime of the country), no damage will be caused to inherent elements of societal vital functions (to human life, health, and property). According to this interpretation, cyberterrorists initially aim to disturb public security, not to damage human lives and health.

Cyberterrorism is a crime against national security and public order because a terrorist's aim is to impose terror upon the society in order to put pressure on authorities and to achieve the set goals.

An object of direct interest to cyberterrorists is information that is stored in computer control systems of a CO. A destructive impact on this system might cause significant losses (damage, after effects) to national security.

Cyberterrorism exerts itself as a threat of violence; it supports a state of permanent fear in order to achieve certain political or other goals, to attract attention to the cyberterrorist's personality, or to the terrorist organization that he represents. Causing damage, or a threat of causing damage, is a peculiar warning of a possibility to create worse consequences if cyberterrorists' demands are not fulfilled.

In research works on cyberterrorism [6], as it was mentioned above, primary and secondary objects are distinguished. Their distinctions are relative. If we use such terms as "primary" and "secondary" objects, taking into consideration peculiar properties of cyberterrorist goals, actions, and consequences, then there is a need to describe each object more precisely using legal language[6].

The *primary object of cyberterrorism* is an information system (equipment, including means of computing facilities, peripheral, communication, television, video, and audio), and information protected by law, which accompanies objects of critical infrastructure.

The *secondary object of cyberterrorism is:*

- an individual, or a group of people, which accompany the primary object, or depend on its exploitation mode, that might be exposed to destructive impact coming from this object and even cause damage to human lives and health;

---

[6] Here we specify primary and secondary objects in legal aspect

- objects of critical national infrastructures that are supported by primary objects and can suffer significant material damage, sustain losses that are hard to renew, social, economic, political, and other types of expenses.

2.3.4. Subject of cyberterrorism

As a general rule, the subject of a crime is an individual of sound mind, who at the time of commission of a socially dangerous action prohibited by the law, has reached the age of criminal responsibility. In the Criminal Code of the Russian Federation the definition of the subject of a crime is not given. In Article 19, general conditions of criminal responsibility are named, among them – soundness of mind, individual entity and age, indicated in the Code.

The subject of a crime is an individual or a group of individuals, who possess the features of the subject of a crime. Due to the complexity of the investigated phenomenon it is worth introducing additional characteristics of the subject of a cyberterrorist crime in the following context.

The subject of a cyberterrorist crime is an individual or a group of individuals possessing the features of the subject of a crime, whose goal is an act of cyberterrorism against an object or objects of critically important infrastructures protected by the law, and who use both open (legal) and hidden channels for data transmission through the internet.

2.3.5. The objective aspect

The objective aspect of the legal violation is a characteristic of a legal activity, which contains such components as time, place, act (action), tool, mode, circumstances of crime realization, size and character of damage (harmful after effects), and connection between the act and the damage.

The objective aspect of cyberterrorism will be an entity of the following elements with their reason/consequential ties.

Time.

The time when a terrorist act of is conducted can affect the number of victims and consequences, depending upon the object the cyberterrorist attacks and what goals he pursues. For instance, an important factor during the realization of a cyberterrorist act is the CO's functional mode (24-hour, night shifts). During an attack against an ecologically vulnerable CO, the chosen time of the year might be of significant importance.

Place.

To define the place of a *cyberterrorist* act is a complicated task, because when the hidden channels of data transmission, and the introduction of bookmarks in the software and other similar modes of committing a crime are used, *the crime scene*, in the narrow sense of the word, can be a *technical means*, through which the act had been realized, and in the broad sense of the word – *the state,* on the territory of which the mentioned technical means - the instrument of the act – is situated.

It is worth mentioning that not only *an object, but also a state against which the cyberterrorists conduct attacks, can be a crime scene. A crime scene is not only a place where criminal actions take place but also a place where dangerous consequences occur.*

The crime scene in acts of cyberterrorism can be defined in multilateral agreements among leading countries as the *territory of the state which has experienced the consequences of the crime.*

Means (tools).

There is no single definition for the term "tool" in the case of cyberterrorism.

A tool of conducting a crime of a cyberterrorist nature is, as a rule, a computer or computer complex on a network base. Information and a computing complex designed for controlling national critical objects can become an object for conducting a crime with the help of criminal tools.

The peculiarity of this type of crime is the fact that harmful software and data (for example, some bit lines), used as criminal tools, can be eliminated "without leaving a trace" by a potential cyberterrorist after performing actions in a certain order.

Mode.

A mode of committing a crime is a combination of methods and techniques that were used by a criminal to conduct the crime. Among them are the following:

- Collection of detailed information about possible objects, their locations and characteristics;
- Fund raising in support of terrorist organizations;
- Creation of web-sites with detailed information about terrorist organizations, their goals and objectives, publication of data on time and place of meetings for those who are interested in supporting the terrorists, guidelines on the forms of protest, etc.;
- Using web-sites for recruiting, considering new candidates, dissemination of information about how to manufacture weapons and explosives;
- Exchange of encrypted messages, various video- and audio-materials through different online chat rooms and forums;
- Familiarization of a mass audience with future planed actions, wide public announcement of "taking responsibility" for acts of terrorism;
- Informational and psychological impacts on the population through computers and other electronic devices;
- Involvement in terrorist activity of accomplices who suspect nothing, for example, hackers who do not know to what their action might lead.

In the context of present research, we will focus only on methods and modes that have been used for destructive actions against critical objects of national information and telecommunication infrastructure. The actions mentioned above are also related to objective aspect of the crime.

Circumstances of crime realization.

Cyberterrorism is a socially dangerous act both in cases when the act of cyberterrorism is conducted in order to coerce a state's authorities to act beyond their legal power and when it is conducted in order to morally and psychologically influence citizens through either overt or covert methods.

Scale and character of damage.

Social danger of a cyberterrorist act is defined by the size and character of losses (casualties, harmful after-effects). Size and character of consequences caused by acts of cyberterrorism can be identified by the following factors:

- Death or injuries to people;
- Property damage;
- Political damage;
- Other socially dangerous consequences;
- Threats to conduct the mentioned actions.

2.3.6. Subjective aspect
Guilt.
Cyberterrorism cannot be conducted through carelessness because this act is initially "aimed" (politically, religiously, ethnically, socially), that is, it has direct intent. Direct intent means that an individual realized the danger of his actions (or inactions), foresaw the possibility or inevitability of socially dangerous consequences but nevertheless desired them.

In this respect, it is worth noting that an act of cyberterrorism cannot be conducted through inactivity. Such an act initially presupposes a certain sequence of actions in order to achieve criminal result.

Motives and goals.
Motives for a cyberterrorist act might be various in nature. One of the possible motives is revenge for unfair or unjustified (from the terrorists' point of view) decisions of government bodies. As a result, the government bodies (including supreme organs) can be coerced to commit actions profitable for terrorists. Personal persuasion can also be such a motive. Motives can be religious or ethnic in their nature. However, in most cases the act of cyberterrorism is considered to be a politically motivated action.

Goals in this case are attempts to solve personal, national, ethnic, political, geopolitical, religious, or economic issues through actions of a cyberterrorist nature. Among these actions, for example, are:

- violation of public security and order;
- intimidation of the population;
- provocation of a military conflict.

Cyberterrorist actions are target oriented. As a rule their targets are objects of national information and telecommunication infrastructure. Among them are hardware means, including computers, peripheral, communication, television, video-, and audio-equipment; software; network standards and codes of data transmission; information that can be presented as database, audio- and video-records, archives; people working in the field of information. A crime's motives and goals are subjects for thorough analysis.

An action (act) of cyberterrorism will be considered a crime, from the moment when socially dangerous consequences occur or from the moment the threat of committing such actions is created.

2.3.7. Environmental position
The term "environmental position" is not a legal term, and is usually used in technical sciences. For its practical use in legal procedure it is necessary to explain how an environmental position is correlated with cyberterrorism. In the theory of systems, *environmental position* is an entity of objects with which a certain system can interact. *Environmental position* is an entity of external conditions in which a certain process occurs.

Under *environmental position in information and computer science* we understand an entity of hardware/software, systemic and other tools which might not be fixed in the system, but are used by developers and users of hardware and/or software that interact or have a possibility to interact with the system related to the given environmental position. Hence, hardware, systems (operational), software, information, communication, and physical environments are distinguished [4]. In our case we are mostly interested in communication environment, which is the most attractive for potential cyberterrorists. Thus, the following legally and technically grounded definition of environmental position can be given.

The *environmental position of a cyberterrorist act* is a complex of hardware, systems (operational), software, information, communication, and physical environments with which an information system interacts in case a cyber attack occurs.

Environmental position, in a broad sense, may include *scene of the crime or scene of the event,* where the criminal act occurred.

The detailed, scientifically and practically grounded analysis of cyberterrorism allows us to include the definitions of "cyberterrorism", "act of cyberterrorism" and other related terms in many glossaries and dictionaries that contain terms of information technology security and information security as a whole, as well as in many legal and technical dictionaries with similar topics.

The Basic Dictionary of terms and definitions in the field of counteracting cyberterrorism can be found below. The definitions are given in alphabetical order and their explanations can be found in the text of this work, in conceptual documents in the field of information security, and in the list of references[7].

Remarks in conclusion. The Basic Dictionary of notions and definitions in the field of counteracting cyberterrorism

"Security (safe functioning of the system, including national and state)" is a condition that exists when a complex of potential internal and external impacts do not take the system beyond the limits of previously formulated conditions that are qualified as safe.

"Secondary objects of cyberterrorist activity" are large groups of people, environment, and various material objects, that can experience *destructive informational impact* to the extent of their elimination, caused by the loss of functionality by primary objects.

"Destructive informational impact" is an unauthorized informational impact on the information system, which either disrupts its functionality or destroys it by violation of its informational-technological structure.

"Information security activity" is a complex of mechanisms, tools, methods, measures and means, that permit prevention, detection, and in case of detection - immediate reaction to the actions leading to destruction of the network environment that supports the COs' function, through damaging of the control system or its elements, and through unauthorized access to the classified information, protected by the law, thereby breaking its entity, structural management and safety.

"Information technology" is a structuralized complex of organizational, technical and technological processes for creating software and computing means for information processing, storage and transmission.

"Infrastructure" is a set of separate inter-related structural elements of a system that support its functionality (assigned functioning).

"Cyberterrorism" is a trend of terrorism that, for achieving its goals:

- uses information and computing complexes and network segments that support critically important systems from the point of view of national security, as objects of destructive impact;

---

[7] In this work, authors focus on a detailed, scientifically grounded definition of cyberterrorism. Other definitions, developed by the authors for The Basic Dictionary, are given with less detailed explanation.

- uses means of computing technology and software as subjects of impact.

"An act of cyberterrorism" is a terrorist act conducted through computer and communication means, the usage of which can either potentially or directly cause danger to people's lives and/or damage to material objects.

"Counterterrorist information security" is a complex of mechanisms, tools, methods and measures that allow the prevention of cyberterrorist activity upon *the primary object*. These measures and tools should include: cyberterrorist activity detection and prevention, as well as assuring the safe function of *the primary object* in case of its partial damage.

"Counterterrorist operation" is a complex of special, military combative (and other) actions using combat equipment, weapons and special tools to disrupt the terrorist act, to neutralize the terrorists, to ensure security of individuals, organizations and establishments, and to minimize the after-effects of the terrorist act.

"Critical infrastructure" is a set of separate, interconnected components that support functionality of Russia's vital spheres.

"Critical information infrastructure" is a set of hardware/software, network, and informational components that support Russia's national vital functions.

"A critically important object" is an object of critical infrastructure, which in the case of partial degradation or complete loss of functions, is capable of directly, and during a relatively short period of time, influencing the state of national security, or some of its components.

"A critically important segment" is a complex of *critically important objects,* united by one or several features such as, for instance, area of application, departmental membership, vital importance, information security demands etc. A critically important sector exists on a higher level in the hierarchy. It characterizes an entity of *critically important objects* and/or *segments,* related to economy, defense complex, social and spiritual life.

"National information and telecommunication infrastructure" is a set of certain hardware/software resources, information components and telecommunication means that support functionality of Russia's vital spheres.

"An object" is a complex of buildings, constructions and technical means with installed systems and tools of informatization, telecommunication and communication, that are located on a common territory, are unified by a certain technological process, has a name and geographic coordinates. It includes economic, administrative or industrial complexes, united by stable ties and task-oriented functionality.

"The primary object of cyberterrorist impact" is understood as:

- computer complex for a relatively limited, but strategically important activity, able to directly influence human life and health, national security, and area of its application;
- large integrated system of distributed information and computing resources for serving nationally important activities (economic sector, industrial sector), for example, energy (including nuclear), transportation (air or railroad) system and its elements (local, regional).

"Counteracting terrorism" is an activity performed by the government bodies and local authorities. It presupposes:

- terrorism preemption, including detection and elimination of reasons and conditions that support commission of a terrorist act (prophylactic measures);

- detection, preemption, disruption, discovery and investigation of a terrorist act (fight with terrorism);
- minimization and/or elimination of the terrorist act's after-effects.

"Information security system" is a set of measures, methods and means that are created and realized to ensure the required security level of an informational resource.

"Country's security condition (nationally safe)" is a condition of the country's functionality (as a large multi parametrical system) when the entity of its characteristics - parameters - are within limits which qualify (identify) the condition as safe.

"Means for creation of a country's security condition" is a set of mechanisms and methods of application (models, scenarios) on the part of governmental bodies (this is one of the main functions of a state) for keeping the country (a large system) in a safe condition.

"Terrorism[8]" is the ideology of violence and the practice of impact on decision making of the governmental bodies, local authorities or international organizations, through intimidation of population and/or other forms of illegal forceful actions.

"Terrorism[9]" - *Terrorism is* the manifestation of extremism through actions, based on disagreements (national, transnational) between separate groups of individuals with government interests and institutions (political, social, on a religious, or criminal basis). Its aim is to create in the society an atmosphere of fear and tension, to form the factors which directly or indirectly destabilize national security with the goal of making demands that cannot be met in the framework of the existing regulatory field.

"Terrorist act" is commitment of an explosion, arson or other action connected with intimidation of a population and endangerment to human life, that causes significant material damage, ecological catastrophe or other serious after-effects, with the goal of illegal impact on the decision making of the governmental bodies, local authorities or international organizations, as well as a threat of committing the above actions with the same goals.

"Terrorist activity" includes:
a) organization, planning, preparation, financing and realization of a terrorist act;
b) instigation of a terrorist act;
c) formation of an illegal military unit, criminal society (organization), organized group for the realization of a terrorist act and participation in this kind of structure;
d) recruiting, arming, training and using terrorists;
e) informational or any other assistance in planning, preparation or realization of a terrorist act;
f) propaganda of terrorist ideas, dissemination of materials or information, calling for terrorist activity or justifying the necessity of such activity.

"Goal of cyberterrorist activity" is the use of a *primary object* (including its network infrastructure) for a *destructive informational impact* on a *secondary object,* with the goal of various after-effects (ground for blackmail, attempt on human lives, ecologic catastrophe, destruction of *secondary objects* etc.).

References

[1] Vasenin V.A. *Information Security and Computer Terrorism/* in Anthology "Scientific and Methodological Issues of Information Security", ed. Sherstjuk V.P., MSU, 2002; (in Russian).

[2]   Vasenin V.A. *Scientific Issues of Counteracting Cyberterrorism*/ in "Mathematics and Information Technologies Security. Materials of the 2-3 November 2005 Conference in MSU" Moscow, MCCME, 2006; (in Russian).
[3]   Vasenin V.A., Galatenko A.V. *Computer Terrorism and Network Informational Security*/ in Anthology "Hi-Tech Terrorism, Materials of the Russian-American Seminar. Moscow, 4-6 June 2001 Russian Academy of Science in Cooperation with National Academies of the USA. pp. 211-224; (in Russian).
[4]   Kazarin O.V. *Computer System Software Security* / Moscow, MSU, 2003, 212p.; (in Russian).
[5]   *National and Global Security. Superterrorism: New Challenge of the New Century*/ ed. Fiodorov-Moscow "Human Rights", 2002.; (in Russian).
[6]   Report on R&D *"Methods and Means of Counteracting Computer Terrorism: Mechanisms, Models, Scenarios, Tools and Administrative Regulatory Solutions"* (2005-BT-22.2/001), IISI MSU, 2005-2006; (in Russian).
[7]   Uspensky V.A. *Works on Non-mathematics. Semiotic Messages to the Author and His Friends Enclosed"* in 2 vol. Moscow, OGI, 2002; (in Russian).
[8]   Federal Law of Russian Federation "On Counterterrorism" of 06 March 2006 Sh5-FZ.
[9]   Federal Law of Russian Federation *"On Alterations in Legal Acts of Russian Federation in connection with the Adoption of the Law "On Ratification EU Council Convention on Terrorism Preemption" and Federal Law of Russian Federation "On Counterterrorism"* of 27 June 2006 P53-FZ.

A Process for Developing a Common Vocabulary in the Information Security Area
J. von Knop et al. (Eds.)
IOS Press, 2007

DECLARATION of the NATO-Russia Advanced Research Workshop "A Process for Developing a Common Vocabulary in the Information Security Area"

This Declaration was adopted by all the participants of the Advanced Research Workshop "A Process for Developing a Common Vocabulary in the Information Security Area".

Harmonization of the national conceptual apparatus is crucial for the further development of the international cooperation in the area of information security/ assurance and counteraction cyber terrorism.

The existing experience in developing information security/assurance, counteraction cyber terrorism and computer crimes glossaries demonstrates the real difficulties and the lack of prospects in working out the common glossary which would cover all the possible applications.

It is necessary to develop more than one glossary in this area. Every special glossary should be oriented to the special customers and should treat conceptions from the different points of view such as scientific, political, technological, legislative ones and etc. There is evidently a necessity in at least four types of the information security glossaries:

Glossary for the international collaboration;
Scientific glossary;
Corporative glossaries;
Glossary for lawyers.

The glossaries should be renewed and corrected with the development of the computer technologies permanently.

The modern network technologies should be used for the developing of the glossaries in order to involve the scientific, business and political elites in this work.

To recommend the Russia-NATO Scientific committee to support NATO-Russia Scientific for Peace Project on the development of the bilingual glossary (Russian/English and English/Russian) on the Information Security/Assurance. This glossary should be oriented for applications on the working out the international documents/agreements on cooperation for the counteraction the cyber terrorism and computer crimes as well for creation the international system of CERT centers.

A Process for Developing a Common Vocabulary in the Information Security Area
J. von Knop et al. (Eds.)
IOS Press, 2007

Author Index